Praise for

YOUR LIFE IN COLOR

"Dougall puts the power of color energy on full display.
This is an informative, fun read that delves into the deeper
meaning behind colors we see every day."

— **James Van Praagh,** *New York Times* best-selling author of
The Power of Love

"Powerful, motivating, and uplifting. The book has helped me
explore different parts of my consciousness using color, enhancing
my ability to tap into my intuitive side in simple ways."

— **Nicole Richie,** *New York Times* best-selling author of
The Truth About Diamonds

"A brilliant yet fun and simple approach to utilizing color energy for
personal transformation. Dougall Fraser's connection to auras
and energy will inspire you to weave more color into every
aspect of your day! Written in his intelligent and witty style,
this is a book that will educate and entertain. Beautifully
rendered and eloquently explained."

— **Colette Baron-Reid,** best-selling author of
The Map and *Uncharted*

"The aura color descriptions that Dougall lays out in *Your Life in
Color* are very detailed and easy to apply to your life. This book
invites you to open your own third eye and start understanding
yourself and the people in your life with more clarity."

— **Glynis McCants,** numerologist and best-selling author of
Glynis Has Your Number and *Love by the Numbers*

"*Your Life in Color* is written in a style that represents Dougall
Fraser's wit, humor, wisdom, and knowledge. Once you begin
to understand and work with colors, understanding how
they affect and influence your life, you'll never
look at them in the same way again!"

— **John Holland,** psychic medium, spiritual teacher,
and best-selling author of *Power of the Soul*

YOUR
LIFE
IN
COLOR

ALSO BY DOUGALL FRASER

But You Knew That Already: What a Psychic Can Teach You about Life

YOUR
LIFE
IN
COLOR

EMPOWERING YOUR SOUL
WITH THE ENERGY
OF
COLOR

DOUGALL FRASER

HAY HOUSE, INC.
Carlsbad, California • New York City
London • Sydney • Johannesburg
Vancouver • New Delhi

Copyright © 2017 by Dougall Fraser
Published and distributed in the United States by: Hay House, Inc.: www.hayhouse.com® • *Published and distributed in Australia by:* Hay House Australia Pty. Ltd.: www.hayhouse.com.au • *Published and distributed in the United Kingdom by:* Hay House UK, Ltd.: www.hayhouse.co.uk • *Published and distributed in the Republic of South Africa by:* Hay House SA (Pty), Ltd.: www.hayhouse.co.za • *Distributed in Canada by:* Raincoast Books: www.raincoast.com • *Published in India by:* Hay House Publishers India: www.hayhouse.co.in

Cover design: Charles McStravick • *Interior design:* Bryn Starr Best

Library of Congress Cataloging-in-Publication Data

Names: Fraser, Dougall, author.
Title: Your life in color : empowering your soul with the energy of color / Dougall Fraser.
Description: 1st Edition. | Carlsbad : Hay House, Inc., 2017. | Includes bibliographical references.
Identifiers: LCCN 2016046663 | ISBN 9781401951689 (tradepaper : alk. paper)
Subjects: LCSH: Color--Psychic aspects. | Parapsychology.
Classification: LCC BF1045.C6 F73 2017 | DDC 133/.25356--dc23 LC record available at https://lccn.loc.gov/2016046663

Tradepaper ISBN: 978-1-4019-5168-9
10 9 8 7 6 5 4 3 2 1
1st edition, April 2017

SUSTAINABLE FORESTRY INITIATIVE
Certified Sourcing
www.sfiprogram.org
SFI-01268
SFI label applies to text stock only

Printed in the United States of America

❖

FOR COLETTE BARON-REID.

Your friendship, guidance, and encouragement have meant more to me than you can know.

❖

CONTENTS

❖

PREFACE

❖

Writing a book is a profound and powerful experience. There are so many people who are a part of this process, and most of those names will be mentioned in the acknowledgments section. There is one person in particular that I must mention before you begin reading.

My husband, David, wrote this entire book with me. After years of working together, we created a concept and process that merges my ability as an intuitive coach with my passion for color and self-help.

Even though his name may not appear on the cover, please know that his soul, heart, and voice are woven into every page.

David, you are brilliant, talented, and an honor to work with every day. Thank you for helping me turn 20 years of sessions into a complete and thorough body of work.

I love you.

INTRODUCTION

❖

I sat in my new optometrist's office as she conducted my eye exam. The wall behind her desk was covered with prestigious diplomas, fancy accreditations, and certificates of excellence. As someone who left high school early and got a GED, I am always impressed by those with a traditional higher education. After successfully reading from the list of letters to test my vision, I braced myself as she dilated my eyes with drops.

"Now remember, Dougall, your pupils are wide open, and you will be sensitive to light for the next few hours after this exam."

You don't know the half of it, I thought. She then asked if I ever saw anything unusual that she should know about.

"Um, well, what do you consider unusual?"

"Like spots, dots, lines, or anything you might see during the day that isn't physically there."

Oh boy. This is a charged question for a psychic to answer. I was there for an eye exam and to renew my contact prescription. But when you make your living as an intuitive life coach, the mere question "Have you seen anything strange lately?" is not going to be answered the way this doctor is used to. In fact, the answer will probably cause her to think that I am all kinds of crazy.

Where shall I begin? In the past week, I saw orange light around a fellow intuitive, a deep green aura coating the arms of a successful author, and a halo of blue energy floating around the head of an attorney. Today, in the doctor's waiting room, the receptionist had opaque, dark blue light all around her arms; this tells me that she suspects her husband of cheating. And there is a sparkle of gold energy in front of my optometrist's shoulders, letting me know she is thinking of leaving this office to start her own private practice.

"Nope, nothing unusual at all!"

She updated my prescription, and I was on my way.

Every year, when I am presented with this question, part of my brain has to ask, *What if the past 20 years of seeing auras and energy was actually just astigmatism?* Can you imagine building an entire career and body of work on a misdiagnosed eye problem?

My parents used to say I would talk about seeing colors above my crib as a toddler. I don't remember this, but I do remember announcing at the age of five that I had a friend who was a ball of pink light named Doshun. My parents were supportive of my "active imagination," but I'm sure that my dad pulled my mom aside to ask if any of her hippie friends had given me their adult brownies by mistake.

I have been able to see color energy around people since I was very young. But I did not initially understand what this energy meant for the people that were surrounded by it. At first, seeing aura colors was just a fun hobby that I enjoyed. My early readings would involve me telling a client what color I saw around them but not offering any true insight from that color. It was as though I could read words from a new alphabet but didn't understand any of the language itself. But as I continued exploring this new language, it spoke to me in ways that I found surprising. It took 18 years of working with clients to hone the messages I was receiving from spirit, and I continue to learn more about harnessing the power of color every day.

As my work with color energy evolved through the years, I have also learned there may be a scientific explanation for the experiences I have had since childhood. I have been told that I exhibit signs of synesthesia, which is when one sense (like sight) leads to an automatic, involuntary stimulation of a second sense (like sound or taste). Essentially, synesthesia occurs when two senses overlap in unusual ways. Synesthetes may describe seeing music, hearing a photograph, or even tasting certain words. In my case, hearing the sound of your voice results in my seeing color around you. And this would have been the end of my experience with hearing color, had it not been for my job and the countless readings I have done for clients. Being an intuitive has given me the opportunity to connect a third sense, which is the feeling, or energy, of each color. Synesthesia may also explain why the colors I see have different meanings from traditional Sanskrit chakra colors or any other color therapy approach. Each color presents consistent properties to me. I am not saying my definitions are the best or only way to interpret color. I encourage you to explore the various approaches to understanding color, but this is how *I* interpret the color energy I see around people.

Here's a quick explanation of how I utilize color when doing a private session with a client: As soon as I hear the sound of someone's voice, I start to see a glow (either physically around them or in my mind's eye if I am on the phone). I believe that when I hear a person's voice, I am seeing the color of their current energy, or, even deeper, the color of their soul. I explain what this color's qualities are as a jumping-off point, and then I use my intuition to tap into how this color applies to my client's specific life path.

My goal for this book is to relay the information about color that I have collected over the years in the hope that you can use it as a tool for self-improvement. You do not need any previous experience with intuition in order to utilize my approach. All levels are welcome! It is wonderful if you believe in energy and the idea of auras. Or if you are just curious about people whose brains process energy and information differently, that's great too. Regardless of your beliefs, there are plenty of historical, scientific, and cultural references within these pages to keep you informed about the power of color.

My fascination with psychic phenomena came as easily to me as some kids take to baseball or ballet. For me, the most interesting thing in the world was anything having to do with spirituality or the occult. After years of therapy and some healthy examination of my life's journey, this fascination now makes perfect sense to me. From the age of 7 until about 19, I was in quite a bit of emotional pain. My older sister was diagnosed with leukemia when she was 16, which rocked the whole family to its core. My parents were miserable in their marriage and began the process of divorce. I was struggling with the deep awareness that I was gay, while growing up in a very conservative town. An even deeper secret was that I was being molested by a family friend. I desperately needed to know there was a purpose, a meaning, behind all the good and bad things that we experience in life.

Sounds complicated, right? I truly believe that my psychological pain cut so deeply that I just needed to focus on something at the time that would soothe me. The idea that processes like meditation, tarot, chanting, or channeling could take me outside of my pain was very seductive. I had created a spiritual form of disassociating. Being bullied at school today? Let's just meditate that away. Mom and Dad are fighting again? Let's try to get a message from our guardian angels. The more spiritual books I read, the more obsessed I became. In the midst of so much uncertainty, the idea that I could predict the future for others and myself gave me a great sense of peace. Saving myself or anyone else from pain became my mission, and color would soon become an integral tool in my healing process.

As I progressed into my teenage years, I became a pretty decent tarot card reader. I was completely devoted to sharpening my intuitive skills. I took courses, workshops, and retreats every chance that I got. At 16 years old, I was not exactly the target demographic for these kinds of experiences. Nonetheless, I felt completely welcomed and supported by my new community of mostly forty- and fifty-something spiritual women.

At the same time, I continued seeing auras around my clients and keeping notes on their qualities. The colors that I saw manifested in extremely specific personality traits in my clients. I studied established methods of color energy, including chakras, which I love and respect. But what intrigued me was that my definitions of color energy often differed from those of the traditional Sanskrit chakras. I did not know what to make of this at the time, but I continued my observations.

By my late teens, I was fully immersed in the New Age community and had slowly started to make a name for myself. It is now nearly 20 years later, and I am so grateful for how much my work and belief system have transformed my pain, as well as the pain of others. Every lesson I share in this book has been tested and found to be effective by numerous clients and in my own personal experience.

Harnessing the power of color can work for anyone. I used to spend my days telling people what color I saw around them. I would describe the color I saw when they said their name, and then observe how these colors would change when they spoke about their job or love life. But after seeing literally thousands of auras around clients all over the world, I started to notice clearly repeating patterns and character traits associated with each color. Why was it that every

5

self-employed person had a yellow or golden color around them? Or if someone had been cheated on, why would I always see a certain shade of blue?

I expanded my studies by taking courses on color therapy, meditation, and color healing. I read countless books because I wanted to know more about color energy. What I noticed was that most approaches to chakra or aura color would describe each color's qualities but would not offer practical advice on how to actually invoke or harness the energy of each color. With this in mind, I took regular notes on what I saw around my clients, offering suggestions on how they could use certain colors if they needed a boost of any particular energy. The colors I perceived around clients meant I could see their strengths and also which colors could be used to minimize those traits that didn't serve them. After years of reading this new language, I finally began to understand. This is how *Your Life in Color* came into being.

Color not only became my language for accessing information with clients, but it also offered powerful benefits I can now share with *you* to use whenever you need to. We are all born intuitive. These colors will give you the tools to make powerful changes in your energy on *your* terms.

Although this book focuses on my intuitive experiences with color, I hope it will inspire you to explore and develop your own innate intuition. Intuitive abilities are often referred to as a gift, but I really don't like that description. To me, the idea of someone having a "gift" conjures up an image of someone who is different or better than the rest of us, and I truly believe we are all born blessed with intuition. Unfortunately, many of us are not encouraged to trust our intuition from a young age. Most people are taught to look outside of themselves for guidance in almost every area. Our intuitive glow fades every time we give our power away, until it becomes so faint we assume we don't have any at all. But it is always there, an inherent part of our life force, waiting to be awakened.

While it is certainly beneficial to gain insight from experts, you should always listen to your own intuition when making a final decision on anything. Strong intuition is the result of putting in the time and effort required to connect with other people's energy in a meaningful way. Having a psychic magically know your sister's name may be exciting in a reading, but it is the *insight* they bring to your relationship that matters most. If the information they receive rings true, use it for your benefit. If not, discard it and move forward. As my friend Alan Cohen says, "Take the best and leave the rest." You have access to the same insight as any other person; it is just a matter of amplifying that inner voice.

Our intuitive abilities can be strengthened just like any other muscle. I teach workshops on seeing auras, and I have literally never had a participant leave without seeing color energy around another person. Commit to an exercise regimen, and anyone can get into their best personal shape.

Not many people hone their intuition because we are taught from an early age to seek advice from outside sources. If we think of intuition as a gift, then it is not something we actually have control over. It's much easier to look outward for guidance, but in truth, the most accurate psychic reading you will ever receive can come from inside of you.

I think we are all gifted. Or more importantly, let's replace the word *gifted* with *connected*. This magical planet we live on is surrounded by energy and blanketed in color messages from the universe. It would seem strange to me if only a select few of us were able to see, hear, or know that energy on a deeper level than anyone else.

To succeed as a doctor, lawyer, detective, investor, or in just about any other job, we must tap into our intuitive abilities. You may call your intuition a "feeling" or "hunch," but for me, "being psychic" simply means that I have developed my intuitive muscles through practice and seeing thousands of clients. It's sort of like the difference between someone who exercises twice a week and someone who is a personal trainer.

What if your own soul was the GPS you could use to consciously locate yourself in the universe and connect to all higher wisdom and understanding? If we each have our own inner guidance system, then color serves as an address on the map of our life. Each color helps us find specific points on the map that we need to get to. Want more leadership qualities? Follow the route toward purple. Need a boost of self-love? Buckle up and head toward pink.

This book is about much more than just understanding color energy. My ultimate intention here is to enlarge your capacity for positive change, using color as a catalyst. What you hold in your hands is a guide to activating the best, boldest, and brightest version of yourself. As Glinda the Good Witch said in the film *The Wizard of Oz*, you've always had the power—you just had to learn it for yourself.

Our journey together begins with me outlining my process of harnessing each color's energy. I refer to this as color activation. But that is only the beginning. In each chapter, we will explore one color to see how its energy can affect you and your environment. We will delve into the historical, cultural, scientific, and religious associations of color to see how they align with the qualities I see. I will tell you about clients who used color to make positive life changes, as well as offering various examples from my own life. By the way, thank you to the many clients who agreed to share their experiences while working with me (some have understandably asked to have their names changed due to the personal nature of each story). I will then lay out step-by-step instructions on how to incorporate color into your life through a series of techniques that have been tested by my clients. I will show you how to activate color in your life through exercises, affirmations, visual meditations, color props, and more. Every technique is designed to be a powerful, practical tool in enhancing your life. I am so excited to share this information with you!

Now let's dig in.

CHAPTER 1

❖

THE ACTIVATION PROCESS

Color activation is the process of harnessing the energy behind each color. When we activate color, we bridge the gap between observing its properties as passive onlookers and actually pulling that energy into our lives for our benefit. This is comparable to watching a cooking show on TV versus actually cooking the meal ourselves. While it is certainly enjoyable and interesting to watch someone else cook, preparing and eating a meal ourselves is a three-dimensional experience.

There are no hard and fast rules for activating color in your life. We all have different senses that are stronger than others, so if you find ways to activate a color that work better for you, great! My ultimate goal here is to empower you, so feel free to take these concepts and make them your own.

Although the approach I offer is a well-rounded introduction to the steps of color activation, I have also incorporated several fantastic options suggested by my clients. Over many years of testing out various techniques, I have discovered the ones that consistently work well and have included them here. The various exercises may change from color to color, but the basic principles of color activation will always come back to the outline you will see below.

I recommend you first try out all the exercises and then gauge which ones resonate the most for you. Each exercise has steps to self-diagnose how you are responding to each color. Again, my goal is to empower your color intuition, so please honor it if certain processes work better for you than others.

Please note: White is the only color in this book that does not involve exercises. The reason I omitted exercises in this chapter is so you can focus on getting familiar with the overall activation process. You are essentially learning to speak a new language of color, and I wanted this first step to be as easy to incorporate as possible. Once you become used to working with color in this way, we will proceed to more involved exercises.

OVERVIEW

Each chapter focuses on a new color, with coordinating activations for each. I suggest initially working with each color for around seven days, but ultimately you should set the pace that feels best to you. It may be tempting to immediately jump around and work with a different color each day, but you need to get used to observing the shifts in your energy and consciousness. Remember, you are essentially learning a new language here. Focusing on one color at a time also gives you a chance to fully understand the subtle qualities of each color's energy.

Color activation falls into the following categories:

1. **Spiritual Activation:** This activation involves meditation as well as exercises to clarify our intention and solidify your soul's connection to the color you are working with.

2. **Universal Activation:** (aka "I spy" with my intuitive eye): When I refer to "I spy," I am talking about the popular children's game that helps pass the time during family road trips. When playing this type of game, you might say "I spy something orange," and then everyone would look around to spot that color in your surroundings. Universal activation involves the same concept of seeking out a specific color in your environment, but in this activation you allow the universe to awaken your consciousness and self-adjust aspects of yourself through signs from specific colors. This involves observing when colors begin to repeatedly catch your attention in an average day. Once you learn to spot the signs, universal activation becomes a fun way to receive messages and guidance. The best part of all is you will be receiving messages from your own higher self, strengthening your intuitive muscles and telling you what you need to focus on in any given moment.

In addition to the activations above, each chapter includes the following tools to help you utilize color:

3. **Color Affirmations:** Color affirmations are a verbal way to align yourself with the energy and intention behind each color.

4. **Physical Activation:** This activation involves using the important concept of color props. Color props are physical objects you intentionally place in your surroundings or on your body so you can see and touch them

throughout the day. Color props serve as reminders that help you to build the energy of that color.

5. **Shadow Sides:** Just like a reversed tarot card, each color has an inverse set of properties. If you find yourself repelled by any color in particular, take a look at the shadow side description of that color. There is a message to be heard.

Each of the categories mentioned is explained in detail below. As you work with *Your Life in Color*, focus on familiarizing yourself with the various activation processes. A reasonable goal is to try to activate color at least once a day during a seven-day period.

Depending on the energy you need most, certain colors may feel very safe and familiar, while others might feel new or slightly uncomfortable. These reactions are completely normal and may evolve as you continue experimenting with color. Pay attention to how your body and senses react to each color. I personally keep a journal when I work with color to note my changing experiences with them. Being mindful of your reactions will provide valuable information as to which energy you need more of (or less of) in your life to achieve balance.

ACTIVATION NOTES

Although the overall activation steps are the same, each color contains unique activation notes. The notes begin with a question that pertains to your relationship with that color's energy. Asking yourself this question will help you assess your current energy in regard to that area of your life. We are all constantly changing and evolving, so I encourage you to come back to these questions whenever you want a current self-diagnosis of your energy. Doing so will give you valuable insight toward your relationship with that color and will help you ascertain the areas of your life that need adjustment.

Enabling practical thought, connecting with your deepest emotional core, empowering leadership skills, and unleashing creativity are just some of the positive traits you can increase through color. It's just a matter of turning the volume up on whichever energy you want to harness.

In addition to the self-diagnosis questions, the notes offer additional thoughts about each color to help you reflect on their qualities. If you ever want clarification on any part of the process, refer back to this chapter.

SPIRITUAL ACTIVATION

You may be familiar with the saying "we are spiritual beings having a human experience," but I tend to forget this by the time I've finished my first cup of coffee in the morning. The distractions of daily modern life are frequent and tempting. I can lose an entire afternoon to my iPhone if I am not careful. I need a regular reminder that at my core, I am energy.

The visual meditation described below is the same one I personally use, and it is what I recommend for my clients. Don't worry, the process does not demand that you meditate for 30 minutes a day in order for it to be effective. In fact, this spiritual activation can be as short or as long as you need it to be. I used to think that to be a spiritual person, I would have to carve out at least 30 minutes daily to sit in the lotus position. I don't know about you, but maintaining absolute mental stillness for this long is simply not a reality for me on a regular basis.

I truly believe even the Dalai Lama hears mental chatter when he is mid-meditation. I assume his mental chatter does not sound like a Valley girl, the way that mine does, but you never know. I used to think I wasn't even meditating correctly if I didn't feel restless and uncomfortable. But let me assure you that when done correctly, your spiritual practice will be a pleasure.

I found that meditating once in the morning gave me a boost of serenity and balance, but these effects would wear off as the events of my day unfolded. As a result, I began testing shorter techniques that were quick and effective for me.

I wanted to be able to center and clear my energy at a moment's notice throughout the day. My intention was to create the meditative equivalent of a nice hot shower that both cleanses my body and revitalizes my soul in just a few minutes. This is important for both mental and physical health; it's a ritual I never question acting upon. My physical showering time can vary. On vacation I may take a longer shower, but on a workday I might hop in and out. But either way, I will have cleansed my physical body effectively.

I would like you to set the same intention for this activation, but for your soul, without any judgment of how long you need. It is terrific if you are able to open yourself to this process for 10 seconds. That means you got 10 seconds of stillness in your day, which is more than many people get. If you can do it for 30 minutes, that is absolutely wonderful. Just do what you can and build from there.

BASIC SPIRITUAL ACTIVATION EXERCISE

I recommend beginners work with the same color for a few days to get accustomed to the process. Each day that you work with the color, spiritually activate it for 30 seconds, or as much time as you need.

My process is quite simple. Years ago in meditation school, I was taught the basic principle *energy follows thought, and thought directs energy.* Basically, the thoughts you focus on will create a shift in your consciousness and soul. I incorporated this idea because it helps us to truly absorb the message of each color. Please note there is no specific color described below so that you can refer back to these steps and easily insert whichever color you are working with.

1. Begin by sitting in a comfortable position. Close your eyes, then take a few deep breaths and bring your attention six inches above your head. As you breathe in and out, envision a softball-sized ball of light there. The ball of light should be whichever color you are working with. I like to recommend that you envision this radiant energy *above* the body to remind you there is something bigger than yourself in your life. I also place it above the body because you are invoking very specific energy from the universe and drawing it down through your body, with the ball of color being the conduit.

2. As the ball of light becomes clearer in your mind's eye, you will begin to notice it growing and pulsing with each breath you take. This pulsing is your higher self, reminding your physical being that you are guided and protected. God, love, light, Allah, Hashem, Buddha, the universe—whatever you want to call it. I am referring to the higher power that exists all around us. We are bigger and more extraordinary than our physical bodies.

3. Now, in your mind's eye, see the ball of light begin to burst like a sparkler, showering your entire being with this bright, radiant light. This light warms you as it washes down through your head, making its way into your throat, expanding in your shoulders, running down your arms and out the palms of your hands. Feel it as you begin to ground this energy throughout your entire physical body. The light moves down your torso, expanding through your waist and hips. The light then washes down through your thighs, legs, and ankles. It finally bursts out through the bottoms of your feet, going deep into the earth. (Note: If sitting in a chair, keep your legs uncrossed with your feet touching the ground. Doing so will help you to fully engage in visualizing energy flowing out through your feet. However, some people prefer to sit on a meditation pillow with their legs crossed in a "criss-cross applesauce" style. If this is the case for you, modify the visualization so that the energy flows out from the base of your spine instead of your feet.

This simple act of activating color energy will trigger something deep inside your soul. This concept is mirrored in many religions, such as observant Jewish men wearing yarmulkes as a reminder their creator is watching over them. Focusing your attention above your body is a reminder there is a bigger purpose than whatever is currently going on in your life.

When utilizing spiritual activation, each color is always located six inches above the head, in a softball-sized ball of radiant light. Many of my clients who are familiar with chakra systems may find this unusual because they traditionally associate each chakra color with a specific part of the body. To be clear, I have a deep respect for Sanskrit chakras and all forms of meditation. My techniques are not meant to contradict any specific system. I just find this is what works for me.

I began studying meditation extensively when I was 16 years old, and most of the techniques I encountered suggested I focus on the base of the spine, moving upward until ultimately directing loving energy up to the universe. But as you might imagine, the universe is overflowing with loving energy. We, the people down here on this planet, are the ones that are love-anemic, desperately in need of an infusion of loving energy. Therefore, we start above the head and move downward.

In this visual meditation, each color is envisioned in approximately the same spot above the head so we can draw that energy down through the body, grounding its qualities evenly throughout our essence. The final step is to push this energy through the bottoms of our feet, grounding us deep into the earth. In this way, we can use meditation to nourish not only our spirit but the earth as well.

UNIVERSAL ACTIVATION (AKA "I SPY" WITH MY INTUITIVE EYE)

Universal activation (aka "I spy" with my intuitive eye) is a fun activation that allows us to play with loving, universal energy and see where it wants us to focus. I believe we are inundated with healing messages throughout the day, but most of us are too busy or distracted to notice. There is a way to take charge of those messages, and this exercise will teach you how to organically seek them out. There are two ways to experience a universal activation:

1. **Intentional:** Your goal here is to be mindful of whichever color you are working with and pay attention to how often you notice it in an average day so you can receive an additional boost of its energy. When using white, for example, you would set an intention in the morning that you want to receive supportive signs from white energy throughout your day. You then get in your car and start driving to work. At a red light, you happen to look at the car next to you and notice the woman in the driver's seat is wearing a white hat along with big white sunglasses. You can use this visual reminder as confirmation of your intention to bring more spirituality and clarity into your life. Then you get to work, go into a morning meeting, and notice your boss has gotten a new manicure. Her fingernails are painted white. In this moment, you can choose to dismiss this as a coincidence or you can receive the extra boost of white energy (clarity and spirituality). The universe is reminding you that you have activated this energy and can have a dose of it whenever you like. I often to refer to this as conscious meditation. These brief moments of color recognition help you come back to your center in what can often be a hectic day.

2. **Spontaneous:** In this approach, set an ongoing intention to remain open to receiving messages from any color's energy. You can write down this intention and keep it somewhere visible, or just remind yourself of your intention in

the morning before you start your day. Doing so allows the universe to highlight the color whose energy you need the most in any given moment. If you start to notice pink all over the place, your higher self may be letting you know you need to be kinder to yourself and less self-critical. As you get more comfortable working with color in this way, you will start to receive messages on how to best care for yourself and your spirit. Our world is so filled with color, and it will become second nature to notice which shades jump out at you, depending on what you need. If you see your color of the week manifesting itself, take a picture of it with your smartphone and watch the signs begin to add up. If you post it on the social network of your choice, make sure to use the hashtag #YourLifeInColor. Aside from giving me a chance to support you, it is a great way to connect with others like yourself who are exploring color energy.

COLOR AFFIRMATIONS

Affirmations (also known as mirror work) involve repeating a positive message to ourselves so that it replaces negative self-talk. This practice was made famous by Louise Hay's fabulous book *You Can Heal Your Life*. I bought that book as a teenager and it has helped me to overcome many self-created limitations. My twist on this idea is to use color affirmations, which involve repeating the intended energy behind the color you are working with. For instance, the color affirmation I suggest using with gold is "I am powerful and stand in my own light."

If you have never tried doing mirror work, it might feel a bit unusual to look in the mirror and repeat positive messages to yourself. And yet those of us who struggle with self-esteem walk the planet repeating awful stories about ourselves constantly. Color affirmations are a powerful way to replace negative thought patterns with more positive, productive messages. The best part is these messages will be augmented every time you see that color in your life.

Look in the mirror and repeat the color affirmation out loud to yourself several times. Make sure to look deeply into your own eyes as you say it. I personally don't think there is a specific number of times you must say an affirmation to yourself, but I do recommend saying it multiple times a day as you work with each color. The more you say your affirmation, the more it will penetrate into your consciousness.

PHYSICAL ACTIVATION

A color prop is any physical item we use to intentionally magnify a specific color's energy. You will be seeing these throughout the book with every color. Physical activation can be done in a very cost-effective way and will easily bring visual delight. I also love that it allows you to really personalize your color experience with items that you already own. You probably already have a favorite green shirt, pink rose quartz crystal, or purple mug. Color props are a fun, physical way to incorporate the energy of whichever color you are using into your daily routine.

1. Select an item you plan to use as a color prop. This can be an item you already own or something new that you purchase specifically for this purpose.

2. Infuse the color prop with your intention by holding it in your hands, closing your eyes, and really focusing on the meaning behind the color. You can also take this moment to say the affirmation listed for that color. For example, with white you would say "I am cleansed by the white light."

3. Whenever you want a dose of the color's energy, touch your color prop and remind yourself of its energy. You can also repeat your affirmation (out loud or in your head) and take a deep breath to draw in more of this color's energy.

4. In this highly connected world, social media is a fun way for us to increase our energy awareness. To spread this color's energy, take a photo of the color prop that you are using and share it online with the hashtag #YourLifeInColor. I love to see the unique ways that people think of to empower themselves through color. Also, I love to interact and will probably respond to you myself!

Finally, I want to clarify my personal beliefs about color props. Although I have used them for years and have witnessed their benefits in my clients, I do not think color props possess some kind of otherworldly power. It is your intention to infuse them with color energy that makes them powerful.

OBSERVING YOUR ACTIVATIONS

When I am working with any color, I like to keep a journal to see how frequently I receive these messages. If you would like to give this a try, get a journal and list the times the color appeared. Make sure to note what you were focused on and how you were feeling in the moment you spotted the color. For example:

> 11:45 A.M.: Ran into Jen as I was taking a break from trying to finish designing my website. I had been feeling frustrated with myself for being so indecisive about the homepage. She was wearing an emerald green sweater. Reminder to trust my creative decisions.

The reason it is important to note how you are feeling in that moment is the color may have a message pertaining to what you are going through.

SHADOW SIDES

As you activate each color, you may notice that some feel really good, while others may feel somewhat uncomfortable. This is completely normal and is in fact a good thing. It means you are challenging your soul's current energy to step out of its comfort zone. If you have ever gone to therapy, you know that certain topics will be painful or uncomfortable to talk about, even though doing so helps you grow. I call this discomfort the shadow sides of colors.

There is a good chance that if you really dislike a specific color, it is because you need to work on yourself in that area and bring its shadow side into the light. The universe is funny like that. Even if we want to avoid facing a certain aspect of ourselves, it shows up in our aura like a traffic signal pointing out what we need to do.

Think of it like starting a brand-new exercise regimen. If you are out of shape and start taking spin classes, your first few days will probably feel awful. You will sweat like a crazy person and may run out of breath. Your body and brain will tell you to stop torturing them. Wouldn't it be more fun to quit this silly program and go watch some television? Of course it would be easier to do that, because challenging yourself to do something new is never as easy as staying in the same place. But if you can just keep going to the spin class for a few more days, your body will adjust. You will discover the joys of an exercise-fueled endorphin rush. Your mood will improve, and you will become healthier.

If you do find yourself emotionally triggered by certain colors, I urge you to continue exploring. You may be close to having a color-fueled breakthrough.

CHAPTER 2

❖

WHITE

QUALITIES: Spiritual cleansing and clarity

SHADOW SIDE: Feeling overwhelmed by responsibility; having difficulty releasing clutter

Providing a burst of spirituality and clarity, white is the universe's all-purpose cleanser. We all have a product in our home that can clean just about every surface. It works in the kitchen, in the bathroom, and on the windows, and can even remove stains from our clothes! White has similar properties in that it helps to neutralize and balance every aspect of our being. White shines so brightly and at such a high vibration that it is the perfect place to begin our journey with color.

I always advise my clients to start the process of working with color by utilizing white. I find it to be the easiest color for beginners to envision because, as Isaac Newton discovered through his use of a prism, white is actually composed of various other colors in the visible spectrum. Therefore, white contains a balanced combination of each color's traits. I have found that everyone who focuses on white will find an element that resonates for them.

White is an important color for almost all major religions, often worn as a symbol of purity. Christian babies wear white

during baptism, and the Pope wears white during public ceremonies. Jewish men wear a ceremonial white linen kittel to
symbolize purity, while Kundalini yogis wear white cotton
caps to help expand their auras and practice mindfulness.
Outside of religion, doctors wear white lab coats to empha-
size their meticulous attention to cleanliness and to instill a
sense of calm competency. I enjoy wearing white when I am
writing, as it clears my mind and primes my consciousness to
share my truth. White is also the color most commonly associated with cleanliness, new beginnings, and the greater good.

White can be used whenever we need to cleanse our
energy quickly, such as while stuck in a stressful traffic jam or
when nursing a cranky baby. It has saved me during a flight,
when the airline passenger next to me decided to paint her
nails. If you are feeling lethargic, uninspired, or run-down,
white can help.

Imagine you want to clean out a cluttered room in your
house. You would walk into the room and turn on the light.
This white light shines on everything, allowing you to see
which items need to be kept and which ones should be
thrown out. This is exactly how it works when we use white
on ourselves. The white light illuminates the parts of our being
needing attention as well as the parts that can be released.

Various cultures incorporate white to symbolize transition. In the United States, brides wear white to invoke a sense
of purity and new beginnings. Most of us look at a radiant
bride beaming at her new partner and cannot help but feel
hopeful at the life they are embarking upon together. In addition, people who survive a near-death experience will often
describe a vision of being pulled toward a white light. In Asian
cultures, white is often associated with death and mourning. I
have many Japanese clients, and some of them are hesitant to
work with white due to superstitious associations with death.

But to me, birth and death are two sides of the same coin. Each event marks the end of one chapter and the renewal, or beginning, of another.

When using white, we intend to create a fresh start in whatever we focus on. White represents a new chapter and a new set of intentions, creating a sense of clarity in our lives.

White was particularly useful for Charmaine, a new coaching client who had made an appointment with me through my website. New clients start with an introductory session over the phone, where we discuss their goals and I intuitively connect with their energy to find the best path forward. The colors I see around them will often tell me the areas where we should focus. At the stroke of 1 P.M., I dial her number to connect for our first session.

"Hello, is this Dougall?" says a soft voice, slightly breaking up on the other end.

"Hi Charmaine, this is Dougall. Are you on a cell phone?" I ask.

"I—don't—have—a landline," she responds.

Cell phones are a growing pet peeve of mine, as clients will sometimes use them to have sessions in the most random places. I've had clients call me from the mall, from a crowded carpool full of people, from the supermarket, and even in line at the post office! But the best way to benefit from a session is to be in a quiet place where you can really focus on the information coming through.

As Charmaine speaks, I can immediately sense that not only is she on a cell phone, but she is also distracted. I can hear the sound of rushing wind as well as a radio playing in the background.

"Charmaine, are you driving right now?"

She immediately bursts into tears. "I couldn't . . . find the time. I have to pick my kids up from school, and I got a late start to the day. Everything feels upside down and . . ."

Charmaine explains her current situation in less than three minutes. I ask her to pull over for a moment so we can focus for a bit. I have always found the first three minutes of a session, whether it's coaching or a reading, are very telling of a person's life. In this situation, we have a client who can't find 30 minutes for herself. She is already emotional, and all I have done is greet her. We haven't even begun the process of working together yet, but energetically, things are already happening. This is the part of energy work that I love. Our life circumstances often bring about the learning process our souls need in order to evolve, all without our even knowing it.

"Okay, I just pulled into my kids' school parking lot. And I have about twenty-five minutes before they come out," Charmaine manages to say through her tears.

"Perfect. Why don't we take a moment and just center our energy together for a minute. Let's close our eyes. Take a few deep breaths in through your nose and out through your mouth. And very slowly, in your mind, I want you to repeat your own name."

Charmaine stays quiet for about one full minute and struggles with my request. "It feels strange to say my own name, like it's egotistical somehow. I'd prefer to say the name of my spirit guide."

"I appreciate that, Charmaine, and normally that would be a great way to connect with higher consciousness, but let's talk about what's going on in this present moment. This is our first session together for coaching, and what I know so far is that you started crying because you clearly have a lot on your plate. You stated you don't have any time for yourself, and that is why you called from your car. You mentioned your life feels upside down, yet once you got to school to pick up your kids, you realized you were twenty-five minutes early. What does that say to you?"

Charmaine starts laughing. "I guess I do have the time. I just didn't realize it because I am always rushing to be early."

"Exactly. This is why I want you to breathe and chant your own name. When we enter into a space for a reading, coaching, therapy, or even exercise, we must first align and center our energy. By repeating our name to ourselves, we connect to our own energy and not the energy of those around us."

During an introductory coaching call, I always ask my new clients what their goals are. They list the parts of their life they would like to change, and together we come up with a plan. Charmaine gives me a synopsis of where she is right now. Recently separated, she has been a stay-at-home mom for the past eight years. Charmaine also takes care of her elderly mother, who lives near her.

"My main goal is to find a career. I don't know what to do with my life. I will be receiving alimony from the divorce and a small settlement, but it's not enough for me to live the life I want to live. I have been out of work for years, and I just feel like I have nothing to offer the world."

"'I have nothing to offer the world,'" I repeat back to her. "Those are very strong words. Is that really how you feel?"

Charmaine starts crying again. "I don't know, Dougall. It sounds terrible when you repeat it, but I have been in a failing marriage for so long. I wanted so badly for it to work, and yet I know in my heart it wasn't right for me. I just can't seem to remember who I am without being a wife or a mom. That is my identity."

As Charmaine explains her life, she instantly becomes a perfect candidate for white in my mind. Here we have a clearly productive and compassionate woman. She is early to pick up her kids and is a loving mother. Even the words she uses to describe her soon-to-be ex-husband are kind and understanding. However, her energy is cluttered with the needs of other people, resulting in a sense of not knowing who she is. What she needs is clarity.

"I just want you to tell me what to do," she says.

I understand her feelings, but my goal with clients is always to empower their innate intuition. "Charmaine, the first thing we need to do is to reconnect with your energy. From what I have heard so far, you seem very overstimulated. You are going through a divorce. You have several people in your life that need your attention, and, most importantly, you need a job in order to provide for your family. Is this correct?"

"Yes, that's right."

"Okay, our first homework assignment is for you to just work with the white light."

I explain to Charmaine that white is the color of spirituality and clarity. White would be perfect to use in this confusing time. Charmaine is so busy with the needs of others that our first focus is to teach her how to spend some time during the day connecting with herself. I instruct her how to activate the white light and ground it through her body.

"After we ground the white light, I think it would be interesting if you asked the color to remind you what you have to offer the planet."

"You mean ask my spirit guides?" Charmaine asks.

People love spirit guides. All day long, I am asked for names of people's spirit guides and descriptions of what these guides look like. So here's the thing: I love the idea of traveling with a spiritual glam squad as much as the next person. It seems totally fun to have a team in the ether supporting me, helping me along my journey, and connecting me to higher wisdom, and to have my archangel spirit guides protecting me from bad decisions.

However, while this is perhaps a controversial statement, I think our brains sometimes invent spirit guides because we subconsciously want to give our power away. We want to believe someone out there is always watching over us and making things happen. And while I do believe a greater power is always protecting us, this universal energy exists *inside of us* and always has.

What I am trying to say is you can be *your own* spirit guide if you are open to it. Ultimately, we are all made up of energy. Our essence, our soul, our vibration are part of a much larger universal framework, and I feel it is the same with our intuition. We are all surrounded by a tremendously loving voice of guidance. It is not broken up into separate entities that only exist outside of us. We can absorb this guidance whenever we want, just like a plant that is nourished by the light of the sun.

Back to Charmaine.

"No, not your spirit guide," I tell her. "You are going to ask the energy, or, in this case, the color that we choose to focus on, for wisdom."

"That's it? That's all I have to do?"

"That's it."

"You know, I have studied this stuff for years; you can give me more or make the homework a little harder."

"But that's the point, Charmaine. You have studied a lot, and it's impressive. However, at this point in your life, you are overstimulated with information. The simple process of activating the energy and asking it for information may be just what you need to reboot your system."

I suggest to Charmaine that throughout the week, every time she sees the color white, she should stop and ask herself, *what do I have to offer the planet?*

The following week when we connect, Charmaine has had a profound discovery.

"Dougall, this was so interesting. I did the meditation every day for about two minutes and then would go on with my schedule. I had no idea how much white I was surrounded by! I would round the corner of my street and see my neighbors' yard full of white roses. I would take a deep breath in my car and ask myself the question you presented. *What do I have to offer the world?* At first, I would just feel peaceful and like I had all the time in the world to get things done; then, toward the end of the week, I had a sort of intense experience. My son had a book report due and had been begging me to buy more printer paper. I was racing to the office supply store, feeling overwhelmed and a little frantic. I walked into the store and found the paper aisle. I looked up at all these packages and felt irritated there were so many options. Heavy thread, white, off-white—dozens of kinds of paper—and suddenly I realized I was standing alone in an aisle, surrounded by white printer paper. Even the word *white* was written everywhere. I took a deep breath, and the smell triggered something inside of me! It's hard to explain, but I had a flashback. I was standing in the teachers' lounge of the school where I used to teach. The smell of the paper, the feeling of it in my hands, used to make me so happy. I loved teaching. I had chills just thinking about it. Of course I have something to offer the world. Of course I have a reason to get back into the workforce. I am a teacher."

Charmaine and I spent the next 30 minutes talking about this revelation. Now, let me explain something. Nothing magical or mystical happened in that store. Charmaine had been busy ending her marriage and taking such brilliant care of her family that she had forgotten about connecting with herself. However, the universe always knows what we need, and it provided ample reminders to her in the form of stressful life situations. This gave her spirit the opportunity to refocus and reflect upon the things that bring her true joy in life. In the end, Charmaine started part-time substitute teaching and then got a job at her kids' school teaching first grade.

What Charmaine ultimately needed was permission to focus on herself. By carving out a small meditation process and reminding herself of her intention during the day, she found that the answer to her question presented itself. In that moment, she became her own guru.

I truly believe we have all the answers to any problem we face, deep within our own being. The concept of working with color is about reconnecting to your innate brilliance and wisdom.

ACTIVATING WHITE NOTES

AM I AWARE OF MY ENERGY?

(Please note: Although every other color comes with a series of exercises, white is the only color in this book that does not. The reason I omitted exercises in this chapter is so you can focus on familiarizing yourself with the basic activation process. Once you become used to working with color in this way, we will proceed to more involved exercises. Please refer back to the activation process in Chapter 1 for further guidance. The steps in Chapter 1 will serve as your template for every color.)

With white, our main focus is on unifying our thought, clearing our emotional field, and optimizing our energy.

When we activate the color white, we clear our consciousness and remind ourselves that at our core we are spiritual beings. It is so easy in life to get lost in our multitasking. Our job, our family obligations, our role with our friends, our bills, our expectations, and our health can take up all of our emotional space. Everything in our life is constantly swirling around in our soul and our aura. So before we enter into any spiritual state of mind, we need to organize and clear our energy.

From personal and professional experience, I can say you really cannot go wrong with white in any situation.

SPIRITUAL ACTIVATION NOTES

It's important to note that even though I talk about white being used for energetic cleansing, I don't think anyone has "dirty" or "unclean" energy. I sometimes hear clients tell me their aura is clogged, distorted, or torn. While I understand that difficult life experiences can sometimes make us feel damaged, I see it from a different perspective.

Think of your soul as the desktop of your computer. If you are anything like me, you leave all sorts of files on the desktop so they are easy to find. I have photos of loved ones I want to post on social media and share with others. I have documents for books, blogs, and even just journal entries I want to reread. Slowly, my desktop starts to get a little crowded. The more files that are "open and active," the slower my computer starts to work. Now, I am the farthest thing from computer savvy—when my computer gets slow, I call my husband, David, to the rescue.

David looks at my computer and immediately notices my desktop is crowded with files. "How can you focus on anything with all this clutter?"

Slowly and with intention, he moves every file into its proper folder and deletes what is no longer needed. Several more strikes of the keypad and suddenly my desktop is clean. Almost immediately, the computer speeds up, as if it can really focus instead of dealing with all that clutter.

This is a perfect representation of spiritually activating white energy in our lives. Just like a computer, we are all brilliant creations performing countless functions and holding on to a variety of information. But instead of storing documents and files, we are emotionally imprinted with information about our past and present. We carry happy moments with loved ones and life events we are proud of, but we also carry painful or stressful memories of things that occurred along our own personal journey.

At any given moment, a number of these life elements can be active or just working in the background of our consciousness. When we have too many of these energy programs working, it slows us down. We can become disconnected, overwhelmed, or foggy. Perhaps you have trouble remembering things, or maybe you have been feeling that there isn't enough time in the day. Guess what? It's time to clear your spiritual desktop.

This is where white comes in. Spiritually activating white is like an energetic shower that refocuses your energy to a more neutral space. As you get used to this process, it will help you quickly return to the most honest, balanced version of yourself before your energy was swayed by various people or situations. White unifies your intention so that you can file away all the distracting elements of your life and refocus on your core. Spiritually activating white should feel like a freeing, cleansing bath of light energy.

UNIVERSAL ACTIVATION NOTES (AKA "I SPY" WITH MY INTUITIVE EYE)

White has a wonderful, cleansing energy and is perfect for us to begin our journey together. Think of white as a fresh start to this new color process. You are connecting to a part of your soul that has always been there, but now you magnify its intensity.

WHITE AFFIRMATION

I AM CLEANSED BY THE SPIRITUALITY AND CLARITY OF WHITE.

PHYSICAL ACTIVATION NOTES

Since white is used for overall energetic clearing, I like to use color props that I can incorporate into my bathing ritual. I do love a nice cleansing shower, so why not combine that with some white color props? For this reason, most of my bath accessories are white. Keep in mind you can have more than one prop. I don't want you to feel you have to commit to just one color prop. In fact, having more than one will only provide you with more opportunities to be reminded of the energy that you are invoking.

Some white color props you could incorporate into your day include:

- **White bath towels.** This is my absolute favorite. As I dry myself, I like to imagine the towel absorbing any last remnants of energy that does not serve me.

- **A white terrycloth robe.** After I am cleansed, I can picture myself being wrapped in sparkling white energy as I slip on the robe.

- **White pillar candles.** Not only do these represent clarifying white energy, but lighting candles also adds an element of ritual that I really enjoy.

THE SHADOW SIDE OF WHITE

As you begin your journey and activate the high frequency of white, you may be reminded of how cluttered your life has been. An imbalance of white often occurs if you have been neglecting your own needs or not engaging in any kind of spiritual practice. You may have been stuck in negativity or limiting thoughts due to life circumstances. If so, this will be highlighted while working with white.

The shadow side of white may manifest as extra attachment to clutter, or it may highlight how overwhelmed you are feeling in this moment. Allow the shadow side of white to remind you of your self-care routine, and how much or how little you are engaged in it. Another way to be proactive toward balancing white energy would be to take some time and do something just for yourself. It could be getting a massage or going to a park for a quiet afternoon.

White is one of the easier colors to explore—even the shadow side. Remember that we are just letting the light in, so shine on!

CHAPTER 3

❖

GOLD

QUALITIES: Goal setting and higher thought

SHADOW SIDE: Selfishness; being socially unapproachable

The color of independence and intelligence, gold is a booster shot of tenacity and motivation. Gold light is used for prioritizing and goal setting. It helps transform all negative thought patterns and replace them with positive, productive thinking. Gold light is seen around entrepreneurs, inventors, self-starters, and people who enjoy being alone.

Gold light invokes self-confidence, independence, and motivation. It is an appropriate color for self-employed people and those who would simply like to assert more independence.

There are many references to gold's regal energy spanning history, religion, and art. In Hinduism, gold is symbolic of knowledge, learning, meditation, and mental development. It is frequently associated with reliability and wisdom, such as with the terms *gold standard* or the *golden years* of our lives. In the Bible, the three wise men gifted Jesus with gold upon his birth, representing his kingship. In ancient Egypt, Ra was the sun god often referred to as the leader of all the gods. Many civilizations throughout history used gold as currency, starting with Asia Minor thousands of years ago. I often see the color gold around clients who are the providers for their families.

Recently, I was invited to speak at an inspirational event co-created by my dear friend Ramey Warren and her colleague Nicole Richie. It was a perfect opportunity to spread positive energy to a mainstream audience, with keynote speakers such as Marianne Williamson. The Oprah Winfrey Network loved the idea and wanted to film the event as a media partner. David and I got so excited when we heard about this empowering vision. He offered to create a website for them, and he set an intention to help in any way possible.

David has been my manager for about eight years now. We are not only a couple but also dynamic and supportive colleagues. Although he is a pivotal part of my business, David normally prefers blending into the background. Because of this, I often get most of the credit, while he is perceived as my assistant. As we evolved together, David wanted to step more into his own personal power and had been activating gold to help himself.

One day, he had a meeting to help plan the event, and I cleared the breakfast plates so he could get ready. We have an unspoken understanding in our house that whenever one of us has a big work day, the other takes care of housework by making breakfast, cleaning up, and the like.

"I'm feeling really nervous, Doogy," David says over breakfast.

"Really? You're going to be great! There is nothing to worry about."

"I just want to do a good job. I kept waking up last night, trying to think of the right color to activate before this meeting. My mind was jumping around. Purple for leadership?

Maybe red would be best to be heart-centered? Or orange could be helpful for balance? What do you think is the best color for me to use today?"

"Gold for sure. It will help you feel independent and confident in your thought. This meeting is about prioritizing goals for the event. If you activate gold this morning, you will organize your thoughts and walk in with the confident energy that says 'I am capable of doing this!'"

"Gold it is," he says.

"I don't own any gold clothing!" he announces a few minutes later from the closet.

"I should hope not. We don't want you showing up looking like an Oscar statue. And you don't have to literally wear the color to invoke the energy. Now that you've activated it, just visualize it and allow it to give you a boost of confidence."

David meditated with gold that morning and wore his grandfather's antique gold watch as a color prop. He relayed he loved touching his watch anytime he wanted a boost of powerful gold energy all morning. The conference was a huge success, and I was so proud to watch David take on a powerful role and proudly stand in his gold light.

This is just one example of how color can play a role in your life. Just like David was nervous before his big meeting, you may be presented with a business opportunity that triggers insecurity. In this case, activate gold, because it will awaken the business side of you. The more you invoke that energy of independence, the more it will embed itself in your being right when you need it.

Gold is traditionally considered a masculine energy in the healing arts, while silver is perceived as a feminine energy. However, in my opinion, these are just gender roles and not truly representative of how these energies work inside of us as people. I believe we are all naturally blessed with a masculine and a feminine side. We all have the ability to access either energy whenever we want, although this may feel like a struggle depending on the culture that we live in.

For better or worse, society tends to view men as being more independent, confident in their opinions, and easily able step into their masculine role. Women, on the other hand, are expected to be more sensitive, compassionate, and generally heart-centered. I want you to know this is an illusion. You have unlimited access to the best aspects of both masculine and feminine energy.

This concept has always been easy for me to embrace because, as a gay man, there are fewer gender roles to overcome. Anyone who is different from the pack knows that difference comes with the potential for judgment from others. But it is also a blessing, because it teaches you to realize other people's opinions don't really matter. As a result, I can easily explore my silver feminine side, such as my emotional sensitivity, my creativity, or any stereotypically feminine trait. But I also enjoy utilizing assertive gold energy, embodying "masculine" business traits if I need to.

You have the power to do the same whenever you like. Pull the energy that benefits you most in any given moment and forget about gender roles. When our masculine and feminine sides are in balance, the other elements of our lives come into balance as well. Together, we will explore both the masculine and the feminine aspects of our soul, giving us the tools to balance our energy in a powerful way.

Gold represents our "masculine" side, which refers to the idea of being self-employed, self-motivated, and more "in your head" than "in your heart." When I see gold energy around someone, they are usually deeply rooted in thought. Their brain serves them in many positive ways.

Gold helps us to be self-sufficient, to set our intention, and, most importantly, to be confident in our ideas. Even if you do not naturally feel connected to your "business" side, there is no reason to avoid gold energy. In fact, that is all the more reason to experiment with it! You may awaken a powerful part of your being that has been dormant and waiting to be activated.

ACTIVATING GOLD NOTES

AM I STANDING IN MY POWER?

Gold has always been a warm, soothing color for me, much like the sun. The independent energy it imparts makes me feel very inspired, but we all have different relationships with color, and you may feel differently.

You can activate gold whenever you need a dose of independence or goal-setting mojo. If you are hoping to land a job interview or manifest a more satisfying career, use gold to bust through any limiting beliefs about the flow of abundance to your life.

A note about gold: Many of my clients are interested in working as coaches, as healers, or somewhere else in the self-help community. If this sounds like you, wonderful! I applaud and support your desire to help others, just as I was personally drawn to the healing arts myself. However, many sensitive people mistakenly believe that spirituality and business are not compatible, as though it is somehow less authentic to deserve payment for your work. This limiting belief is unfortunate, because it can keep you from turning your passion and talent into a viable profession. If any part of you does not feel deserving of payment for your healing work, it is a classic sign you would benefit from working with gold energy. Please let me assure you, life will become more fulfilling and effective when you are properly expressing both your spiritual power *and* your business identity.

On the flip side, as a practitioner, I can completely relate to the desire to help people who may not be able to afford my services. For this reason, I always work with a limited number of clients for free. I also find this helps me release any blocks to achieving abundance. I recommend working with a few clients per month on a complimentary basis, as you activate gold to help manifest the business you want.

SPIRITUAL ACTIVATION NOTES

Visualizing gold in meditation highlights our own power of thought and the way we carry ourselves. When activating gold, I like to see this energy as a golden sun above my head, leading my thoughts and desires into reality. If I am in a business meeting, I invoke gold to draw its energy to the surface of my consciousness. I use gold when I want to feel confident, capable, and like a master of my destiny.

Gold is an extremely intellectual color, and I sometimes feel my head begin to tingle as I visualize it and sense it increasing my higher thought and independent energy. Your mind may also begin to quicken, which is completely normal with gold. It may also feel as though you are "turning inward" as your mental vibration increases. Do not mistake this for distraction. It is simply your mind reacting to an infusion of gold and rising proportionately. With gold, you activate your mind's power, your inner strength, and your wisdom. This color will help you brainstorm all kinds of new ideas. You are awakening the most powerful, intelligent, driven part of your being.

SPIRITUAL ACTIVATION EXERCISE: JOURNAL YOUR POWER

The purpose of this exercise is to reframe your thoughts in a more powerful, purposeful way. We all have wandering thoughts. Naturally, on an average day, some of your thoughts will be positive, while some may be negative and heavy. You may not even be aware of it, but consistently negative thoughts in your head can affect the outcome of your day—and your life. This is why you want to direct your consciousness toward a positive, empowering mind-set.

1. Before spiritually activating gold through meditation, take a journal or notebook and write down a goal that you have. This should be something you can take action steps toward achieving. For example, you might write, "I want to learn a new language." Your goal can be as big or small as you want. Keep your journal or notebook nearby.

2. During your visualization, think of a quality in yourself that would serve the goal you have set. For example, you might think, *I have a wonderful memory and rarely forget a name. This would be useful while studying a new language.*

3. Under your goal, write your positive quality down in your journal. Then write one thing you can do today to utilize that quality in achieving your goal.

4. Share your goal and positive trait with a friend. Gold energy is very independent, so you want to maintain your connection with loved ones as you use it. Sharing your experience will also help to hold you accountable in working toward your goal.

UNIVERSAL ACTIVATION NOTES (AKA "I SPY" WITH MY INTUITIVE EYE)

Living in this modern world, it is very easy to feel like you have a lot on your plate and to become overwhelmed. With this in mind, it is also very easy to let your goals, and therefore your action steps, fall to the wayside. With each activation, pay attention to where gold energy manifests in your waking world, as a sort of reminder. Every time you see the color in your daily life, it will stimulate this reminder to help your being take back some control. While this takes practice, you will begin to regularly notice where the universe repeats this energy back to you as a message.

When activating gold, you may start to notice it "randomly" in a store, at a friend's house, or even in a passing car. Every time you see and notice the color gold, you reaffirm your intention to strengthen your independence and higher thought. The universe is not only reminding you of your power, but it is also giving momentum to your intention.

UNIVERSAL ACTIVATION EXERCISE: MERGING THOUGHTS WITH WORDS

As you know, I am a big fan of doing mirror work. Sometimes our negative beliefs are nothing more than patterns that have been created in our thinking. Using a gold affirmation is a powerful way to retrain your mind, and this exercise will get you in the habit of repeating that message regularly.

Anytime you notice gold throughout your day, repeat your affirmation silently in your mind. You can use the affirmation listed above; this one would work as well: *Gold light brings my potential into reality.*

Have fun with this one! One of my favorite ways to increase my sense of personal power is to remind myself of it whenever I see gold. This is a simple way to regularly take note of yourself and your greatness.

GOLD AFFIRMATION

I AM POWERFUL AND STAND IN MY OWN LIGHT.

PHYSICAL ACTIVATION NOTES

Gold energy is a unique vibration in that it is more physical in nature than etheric, meaning it inspires taking action. But at the same time, because of its root in thought and the mental body, it really helps us to align with our highest vibrational thinking. When we use gold to unify our energy for any goal, we become effective both physically *and* mentally.

When using gold color props, I like to use items that can be incorporated into physical activities where I can think. This might include exercises such as stretching, taking a walk, or going for a run.

Some gold color props you could incorporate into your day include:

- **A gold ring or other jewelry.** Wearing jewelry is an easy way to harness gold energy. If you own gold jewelry, this is a great time to wear it. Look at or caress it during the day, and you will reactivate its powerful energy.

- **Makeup.** Playing with gold makeup is an excellent way to work with this energy, as you will see it anytime you look in the mirror. Apply it with the intention of invoking gold energy.

- **A gold keychain.** This is a perfect way to always remember your color prop, because it will be in your pocket or your purse whenever you go out.

PHYSICAL ACTIVATION EXERCISE: ACTION STEPS

An action step is any kind of concrete activity that will help get us closer to our goal. Although I strongly believe in the power of positive thought, I also think the manifesting process becomes stalled if we do not pair these thoughts with real, physical steps. Gold is the perfect catalyst for launching our ideas into physical reality. Manifesting a dream job requires more than just lighting an abundance candle, facing east, and visualizing it happening. Believe me, I know, because I have tried this approach and it did not work!

After a while, I observed that the universe speeds up the manifesting process if it sees us take physical steps toward our goal. I can't even count how many psychic fairs I worked at before building my practice into what it is today. Do not allow your ego to stop you from taking opportunities that will get you closer to realizing your soul's purpose. It may seem like you are only taking one step at a time, but you are being propelled faster by the universe moving under your feet.

I believe this is one of the main challenges of our lives. We must learn whether we can rise above our limiting thoughts and accept our potential greatness. Manifesting is like baking the perfect cake. You need the right mix of ingredients to make it rise into what it is meant to be. And gold light is like adding baking powder to the cake, which helps it to rise.

1. Think of something you hope to achieve, create, or receive in your life. Mentally hold this idea in the gold light as you think of it, and then write it down *on paper*. Do not just set the intention in your mind. You must physically write it down as the first step toward grounding the idea in our physical world. Put this piece of paper somewhere prominent, where you will see it regularly. You can tape it on your fridge or perhaps your bathroom mirror. Feel free to tell loved ones about your goal or desire.

2. Select a gold color prop that you can use for this exercise. You can change props as often as you like, but make sure that you have something to use for physical activation.

3. Take steps to accomplish this goal during the next seven days. It is a good idea to start with something simple, such as getting new business cards, registering a website domain name, or enriching yourself with a new class. The idea is to express a goal and take action to fulfill it. Any goal that has been lingering in your mind

will become positively energized with gold, and taking action steps will tell the universe you are ready to receive the fulfillment of your goal *now*. Remember, every bit of effort you make pleases the universe. Baby steps do add up!

THE SHADOW SIDE OF GOLD

Gold's shadow side is that its independent energy can lead to loneliness when overused. Many people who naturally lean to gold energy have trouble connecting with others on an emotional level. This is why highly successful business owners are often unhappy. The same energy that gives them drive and confidence can also lead to social isolation, even from their spouses or loved ones. On the one hand, gold energy provides the fearlessness to make great things happen. On the other hand, when we are in the shadow side of gold, we can come across as cold, ostentatious, and ego-driven.

With the gold light, you will notice your mind doing a lot of brainstorming. This is a chance for you to access this color's energy and get things done. But you may also find yourself wanting to be alone more. Be careful not to alienate yourself from loved ones.

Think of activating gold energy like swimming in the ocean with a snorkel. Your snorkel is an amazing tool, allowing you to look down and be inspired by all the vibrant sea life you discover. But once you have absorbed all that inspiration, look up, take the mask off, and get back in the boat so you can excitedly tell your friends what you saw. Otherwise, you will be surrounded by all that beauty yet completely alone and cut off from other people.

CHAPTER 4

❖

SILVER

QUALITIES: Feminine aspect of God; wisdom and home

SHADOW SIDE: Lack of compassion; imbalanced home energy

Just like the moon, silver holds powerful divine feminine energy. Silver and the moon are often closely associated in popular consciousness, as you will see shortly. As the yin to gold's yang energy, silver is very effective for increasing a sense of security in your life, particularly in your home. Feminine silver has a very stable energy that makes me feel safe. Just as a mama bear protects her cubs, silver naturally protects your family and home turf.

Silver has an established history of being associated with feminine power, as well as the moon. In fact, many moon goddesses have been revered in mythology for their power throughout the world. In tribal societies, the moon, and therefore silver, is traditionally associated with divine feminine energy. The Hawaiian goddess Hina, the African goddess Gleti, and the South American goddess Chia are only a few examples of powerful feminine silver warriors. Artemis, one of the most respected of all the ancient Greek goddesses, was

symbolized by a silver crescent moon. She was the protec-
tor of nature, animals, and young girls, as well as women in
childbirth. In ancient Roman mythology, Luna was the celes-
tial embodiment of the moon and was considered to be the
feminine component of God. Many of the moon goddesses
throughout the world are also associated with protection and
higher wisdom. Luckily for us, we can utilize these qualities
anytime we want through a boost of silver energy.

In the science world, silver ("Ag" on the periodic table) is
one of nature's precious metals, but it also has qualities I find
symbolically similar to silver energy. Silver metal is both strong
and malleable, molding itself to best suit what is required of it
in any given situation. As such, silver energy offers us powerful protection as well as the safety and support we sometimes
crave. Silver metal has the highest thermal conductivity of
any metal, meaning it literally can handle more heat than any
other metal in nature. Using its energy will help concentrate
both your strength and your inner wisdom, until its brilliant
light encompasses everything in your life.

Silver possesses a natural reflectiveness, and seeing yourself mirrored back in silver's power allows you to be elevated
into its wisdom. This is exactly how I feel about feminine silver
light: the more you utilize and pay attention to it, the brighter
this shimmering energy will shine in your own life.

There are also symbolic associations between silver and
the sacred energy of home. One of my favorites is the silver
anniversary, celebrated on the 25th year of marriage. On this
anniversary, couples traditionally exchange gifts of silver as
a sign of fidelity and love. Interestingly, the entire tradition
of anniversaries began with silver and dates back to the Holy
Roman Empire: husbands would present their wives with a
silver wreath on their 25th anniversary. Although it is now
popular in the United States to give gifts for every year of

marriage, silver (for 25 years) and gold (for 50 years) are the most commonly observed worldwide.

The idea behind the silver anniversary is that silver is both valuable and long-lasting, so a silver gift symbolizes a long-term investment in a couple's life together. With this theme in mind, monarchs in many countries celebrate a silver jubilee to mark 25 years of reigning. Silver is the perfect energy to mark the stability and safety of where you are.

Your home is a reflection of your consciousness. I say this frequently and believe it to my core. This concept is also closely related to your relationship with silver energy. What I mean is the way you treat your living space is directly related to how you feel about your life in general. Let's explore your relationship with silver and look at how it may be affecting your home energy.

Imagine that, in this very moment, a new friend calls you unexpectedly. They are in your neighborhood and would like to stop by your house to say hello. How does this make you feel? You may respond with joy and enthusiasm at the prospect of seeing your friend. You might immediately invite them over and feel loving, energetic expansion at their arrival. Or you might tell them that you need a few minutes and then quickly clean up various messes around your home. Your home might be dirty or there might be items lying around you do not want them to see. Or you might find it easier to just avoid the interaction entirely and tell them you are busy. What you want to look at here is the feeling and energy behind your answer. Do you feel *proud* of sharing your home with other people, or do you feel something different? That feeling is being absorbed by your consciousness whether you know it or not.

Your reaction to someone entering your space says a lot about your relationship with silver energy. Of course, it is completely reasonable for you to feel somewhat uneasy in this moment. Your home is probably a bit messy because you were not expecting guests. But I am more referring to your *overall* attitude about having people in your personal space. If you struggle with this idea, working with silver will empower you to both protect *and* open the energy surrounding your home.

I have to be honest: In the past, silver has been a tough energy for me. In my earlier years, when I was faced with the idea of having unexpected guests, I often felt anxious and hesitant about it. Although my living spaces were pretty neat at first glance, I had a tendency to stuff things in drawers just to get them off surfaces and out of the way. I had thought this need to clear clutter was partly due to how sensitive I was to the energy of a space, or perhaps it was the Taurus in me that liked things to look a certain way. But open a drawer or closet door in my apartment, and it would be bursting with random items that were being neglected. When David and I were first dating, he came over to my apartment in NYC, opened the freezer door, and said "Um, why is there unopened mail in here?"

Looking back, I think that this silver energy imbalance stemmed from my parents getting divorced when I was an adolescent. Their irreconcilable differences made separation the right choice for them, but the stability of my home had been taken away at a formative time in my life. I ended up moving out on my own at the age of 17, saying that I craved my independence, but what I truly craved was the home sanctuary I had lost. I just had not fully processed all of it at that point.

This is, I think, why I ended up stuffing things in drawers, much as I had stuffed away the pain of losing parental unity. The shadow side of silver was presenting itself in my life. Having a clean and tidy home was one of the few things I could control at that time, but I only knew how to keep things orderly on the surface.

My experiences with my mother around this time also contributed to my complicated relationship with feminine silver energy. I love her, but my mother has always struggled with boundaries. In my late teens, she fell in love with a person who was severely alcoholic. This was a very difficult time for me, as the family was already dealing with the fallout from my parents' divorce. I was living with my mom in New York when she began volunteering at a shelter for the needy, which is where she met and fell in love with Jorge. I couldn't understand her attraction to someone who struggled with such a debilitating addiction, and I ultimately felt like she was choosing him over me at a critically vulnerable point in my life. In retrospect, I think she just wanted to feel needed and desired.

At the time, we had a bit of a role reversal, and much as any parent would, I vocally disagreed with her choice of romantic partner. I think for children of divorce, seeing your parents date and fall in love with someone new can be awkward. It is even more difficult when they choose someone who is so obviously unhealthy for them.

I had hoped that my mom and I could reestablish a sense of home after my parents' divorce was finalized. I still yearned for that protective silver goddess energy we all want from our mothers. I craved that sense of support and nourishment, but my mother simply could not provide it. It wasn't intentional on her part, but due to her circumstances at the time, she was focused on caretaking for her new partner and was unavailable for me.

If you have a loved one who has struggled with addiction, you know how profoundly it will affect your life when they are dealing with an issue like this. When they are fully engaged in their disease, their home will have chaotic, unpredictable, highly imbalanced silver energy. I wanted to live with my mother, but I just didn't feel safe when Jorge was there.

They lived together on and off, depending on his level of sobriety. Coming home from school, I never knew if he would be the sober version of himself or completely drunk and out of control. The pain of seeing them together was just too much for me to bear, so I moved out on my own. I left New York and moved to Dallas, to be near where my sister lived.

After I moved out, I began activating silver for the first time, to see if I could improve my relationship with my mother. On one trip back to visit my mom, I decided to focus on the safety and boundaries aspect of silver and take care of myself. Regularly visualizing silver, I had come up with the idea to stay at a nearby bed-and-breakfast instead of staying with my mother and her partner. This was a bold move for a kid my age, but I had established my independence and was trying to protect myself. She was hurt by my decision, and in the most polite way I could, I tried to explain that I just didn't feel comfortable with Jorge there.

I checked into the bed-and-breakfast and was greeted by the owner, a lovely woman in her early sixties named Jan. She served chamomile tea in floral porcelain teacups, along with a plate of butter cookies, and told me I reminded her of her son. To me, she felt like the literal embodiment of silver energy. When I finished my tea, she guided me up the grand staircase of her home, which was built in the late 1800s.

"This is a very safe neighborhood, but we do lock the doors at ten o'clock just to make sure everyone feels nice and snug. Here is a key to the front door, in case you come in later than that. Breakfast is at nine o'clock. I hope you like pancakes and eggs. Please let me know if you need anything."

As she quietly closed the door to my room, I looked around with a mix of emotions. Part of me wished this could be my mother's home, but the most dominant feeling I had in this cozy room was that I felt safe. I sat on the antique four-poster bed and felt the soft cotton quilt underneath me. On the nightstand was a glass carafe of water that rested on a round silver tray. Opposite the bed was a fireplace, and on the mantle were four photos of her family in silver frames. Everything in the room had love and intention. I had been visualizing silver prior to this trip, and I noticed that seeing it in my surroundings reminded me of its energy. This was one of my earliest experiences with spontaneous universal activation.

Taking in my surroundings, I realized this was a physical representation of what I was looking for. The silver light helped me release the expectations I had for my mom and realize that I could receive this energy from other sources. It gave me the power to love her without condition and to also realize my own needs and boundaries. I had been focusing on silver in the hope that it would somehow change my mother, but it ended up changing me instead. Activating silver also empowered me to take an honest look at the imbalances that existed in my home.

Silver energy helps us understand that home is about feeling nurtured, safe, protected, and, most importantly, welcome. It is about honoring our sacred space but not creating perfection, which is a lesson I also needed to learn (see the shadow side below). At its best, silver helps us access a sense of community and support through our home.

Finally, here is some food for thought about silver: When I talk about "feminine" energy, it literally has *nothing* to do with your gender and *everything* to do with who you are as a unique being on this planet. We all have masculine and feminine traits. Both silver and gold help us find the balance between our masculine and feminine energies. Don't let gender roles keep you from exploring both of these colors equally. My hope for you is that by working with both silver and gold, you can maximize the best aspects of both energies inside yourself.

ACTIVATING SILVER NOTES

HOW BALANCED IS MY HOME LIFE?

How much energy is coming into your home, and how much is going out? When you activate silver, it will highlight the balance of energy of your home. Are you neglecting the upkeep of where you live? Or are you overly controlling of it? Are you rarely at home, creating your happy memories elsewhere because you hate to be alone? Or do you spend *too* much time at home, isolating yourself in your safe space and not inviting others into it? If you are a natural host, silver will help guide you in expanding that energy in healthy ways. On the other hand, if you are hesitant to share your home with others, then silver will help you see the energy behind that.

Silver goddess energy helps us to recognize the importance of community and home. Typically I see those things as existing separately, but silver has taught me how important it is for them to balance and co-exist. The way we care for our home and how we welcome people into it is also directly connected to the law of attraction. The welcoming energy of silver helped me manifest some of my most meaningful, joyful friendships.

After our wedding in New York City, David and I packed up our apartment and moved to Los Angeles. We loved the sacred silver energy that we had cultivated in that New York apartment, but we were ready to have more living space. Our work brought us to Los Angeles two to three times a year, and moving seemed like a great opportunity to live in a house rather than an apartment. For the same amount that we paid to live in our 600-square-foot NYC apartment, we rented what felt like a palace in Los Angeles.

"It is 81 steps from the kitchen to the bedroom! Does that count as going to the gym?"

"What? I can't hear you!" David would jokingly yell from the kitchen.

We loved our new living situation, but we did not yet have a soul group in our new city. We had a small, rewarding circle of soul-mate friendships in New York, and we wanted to put down the same kind of roots in LA. We decided that part of opening silver energy in our new home would include saying yes to any kind of social invitation. Seriously, someone at the checkout line in the supermarket could have invited us over for coffee and we would have said yes.

I strongly believe the universe likes to see us make an effort before giving us our desire, so I knew I had to make an effort to create a new circle. I would foster feminine silver energy by calling every work acquaintance I knew in LA to see how we could make friend connections with people.

When activating silver, I intended to create a safe, stable community in our new city. I knew I wanted to foster more silver energy, and as we unpacked I visualized us laughing around a dinner table with good friends. A few days later, I scanned through the contacts in my phone and came across the name Marilyn Kentz. A lightbulb went off in my head. I had known Marilyn peripherally through work friends for several years. I didn't know her well, but I knew she lived in Los Angeles, and she had always been friendly, so I took a chance. I sent off an e-mail to her saying we had just moved to LA and would love to meet for lunch or something like that. Within 10 minutes, the phone rang.

"Hello?"

"Dougall, it's Marilyn Kentz. I just got your e-mail, and I think you live around the corner from me!"

Marilyn and I spent the next 10 minutes chatting about how funny it was that we lived so close to each other. I moved across the country and had no idea we would end up being neighbors. I explained that David and I had just gotten married and were having an adventure by moving to Los Angeles.

"You just got married! Then it's final. You are coming over for dinner tonight! I'm chilling champagne as we speak. Do you remember Ramey?"

"Of course I remember Ramey." Ramey was the mutual friend who had introduced Marilyn and me.

"Well, she lives across the street from me, and I am calling her right now."

I got off the phone and told David we were going to a dinner party in an hour. I can't explain what an exciting, big deal that was. It was mind-boggling to me that Marilyn could be that spontaneously generous and hospitable. We were acquaintances, but I'd never invited her to my house and I'd never been in her house. And yet, 15 minutes after one quick e-mail, here she was welcoming us into her home and wanting to celebrate.

That night, as we sat outside enjoying the cool Los Angeles breeze and marveling at her citrus trees, I knew activating silver energy in our new home had paid off in a big way. Marilyn and Ramey have turned out to be some of our closest friends, helping us foster a community and family in Los Angeles. To this day, inviting Marilyn over and sitting around a dinner table laughing is one of the most joyful expressions of silver energy in our lives. Marilyn is also a perfect example of healthy silver energy. Protective of her friends, yet welcoming of new ones, she has set a great example of how to use a home as a tool for fostering a stable community of loved ones.

SPIRITUAL ACTIVATION NOTES

In your mind, scan your house right now and try to gauge how much of yourself is truly reflected in it. Does it feel reasonably cared for and infused with your love? Take a look at the walls and see if there are personal photos or works of art that bring you joy. Ideally, there would be decorations and knickknacks that are imprinted with your unique personal energy. To a stranger, it should look as though you tend to your home. Your bathroom should be reasonably clean, and you hopefully change the sheets on your bed with some amount of regularity. You know you've got a healthy relationship with silver if your home is set up in a way that won't bring up shame for you should someone see it.

Please know, I am not saying that your home needs to be in perfect, tidy condition at all times in order for you to have a healthy relationship with silver. Heaven knows that sometimes I would rather curl up on the couch with a book than fold laundry or take the clean dishes out of the dishwasher. I am saying, however, that the overall way you tend to your home reflects your attitude about silver and about your life in general. If you don't feel like your home is a sanctuary that is being honored, then your relationship with silver energy may be muted or out of whack. If your home is neglected, then there is a chance that other elements of your life are being neglected as well. On the flip side, being overly meticulous to the point that it causes you to avoid having guests (like I used to be) indicates you should work on relaxing your grip to heal this imbalance of silver energy.

If you lean toward being an introvert, like I do, you may shy away from the idea of hosting a dinner. But you must invite your loved ones over once in a while to have a fully balanced relationship with silver. The idea is that we can be protective of our sacred space and still allow our friends to fully integrate into our tribe.

A critical element of healthy silver energy is having your soul group come over and help you cultivate that loving "homey" energy. If this makes you terribly nervous, you could invite just one friend to come over. If this seems easy for you, then really run with it. Think of inviting a new mix of people over. Try to think of someone you know who is looking to make more friends and invite them to meet your other friends. This is a great way to let silver goddess energy pour through you. If you love to cook, then cook for people. If you don't like doing those things, or get stressed about it, have friends over and just get take-out. This is more about the energy behind your welcoming people into your space than it is about actually cooking for them. You will know you are properly activating silver if you feel more safety and love in your home.

SPIRITUAL ACTIVATION EXERCISE: CREATING SACRED ENERGY

Since your home is such a big part of balanced silver energy, it is important to help create a sense of love in it. This is one of my favorite exercises, as I absolutely love making our home feel welcoming and warm.

Your goal for this exercise is to do your spiritual activation in the midst of a "homey" activity: something relaxing that truly symbolizes home for you. The range of activities are almost endless, but here are a couple of examples:

- Light candles, dim the lights, and play your favorite music.

- Take a relaxing bath.

- Prepare a healthy meal.

Try visualizing silver while you enjoy your activity, building a sense of home. Envision a molten, almost liquid consistency to silver as you spiritually activate it. My clients sometimes report that silver feels like a glossy coating on their bodies. It should move through you more slowly than other colors when you see it in your mind's eye. To me, this has to do with the protective, home-balancing intention of silver. Like a long, satisfying hug from a best friend, silver will love and embrace your core. Try taking extra time when you spiritually activate silver. This goddess energy is powerfully protective and deeply profound.

UNIVERSAL ACTIVATION NOTES (AKA "I SPY" WITH MY INTUITIVE EYE)

As we saw earlier, silver is often referenced with the moon in conjunction with goddess energy, while the sun is used as the reference for gold, masculine energy. The sun is bright and intense and can be a little too much at times. But think of the moon—no one has ever said that the moon is too bright or that they got a moonburn from too much moon. The subtle power of the goddess and silver energy are the same. They are always there, guiding us when we may not even realize it. Try to take some time to look up to the moon—to activate and have awareness of this different part of you. When you see silver in your life, you are connecting to your own nourishment. You are invoking a sense of protection and sacred space.

Although universal activations involve items we see when we are out, silver primarily relates to our home, which is where I have focused these notes. You can still activate silver to affect your interaction with others, but this particular activation offers us the opportunity to examine our home and personal space.

UNIVERSAL ACTIVATION EXERCISE: INVESTING IN YOUR SURROUNDINGS

Human beings sometimes put things off when it comes to household chores. When we tend to our home and honor our space, it magnifies our self-love and the energy we project to the planet. Think of a budget you might have in mind for minor home improvements. You could paint a wall, buy new drapes, replace a shower curtain. To be really low budget, you could just clean out that neglected hall closet. Select something simple in your home, and then finish that project. Remember, this is a form of meditation, a way of infusing love, silver protection, and honor into your space.

Take a simple walk through your home. Pay attention to details that need to be taken care of. What are minor issues that you have been putting off for a rainy day? For example, last month we had a handyman come over to do a few small jobs. The switch plate needed to be replaced in the bathroom. There was a light fixture we wanted added to a hallway. We also asked him to wire some café lights on our patio, and he painted an accent wall in our office. For less than $200, we tended to our sacred space, and the feeling after the work was done was so euphoric. These were minor things that needed to be adjusted, but you would have thought that we added a pool based on my reaction. I felt our home was being honored, and the silver energy was flowing so beautifully that day. I encourage you to make a list for yourself and do the same.

Anytime you notice silver, wherever you are, allow it to remind you of an item on your list that you can accomplish this week. Use the silver activation as a motivator to pour love and care into your home.

SILVER AFFIRMATION

I AM PROTECTED BY THE LOVING EMBRACE OF SILVER.

PHYSICAL ACTIVATION NOTES

One of my favorite ways to activate silver is by setting a table for a meal, particularly if we are having guests. Since having friends over allows me to give and receive that loving silver energy, I enjoy selecting a tablecloth with intention and incorporating silver energy into the environment where we will be sitting. Silver napkin holders, silver serving spoons, and silver candle holders are all ways that I can infuse silver intention into a room. I might pick lemons from our tree and place them in a silver bowl for sight, color, and scent. I will set the table way ahead of time, because it makes me happy to look at it. My intention while preparing for my guests is to create a welcoming, relaxed, loving atmosphere so that they feel honored.

Some silver color props you could incorporate into your day include:

- **Silver picture frames.** This also allows you to showcase your loved ones to build that loving silver energy.

- **Silver tray or platter.** One of my favorite color props is a reflective silver tray with glass or crystal candle holders on it. The reflection this creates when the candles are lit makes my heart sing.

- **Silver jewelry.** A silver bracelet or ring is a great way to invoke protective silver energy throughout your day.

PHYSICAL ACTIVATION EXERCISE: HONORING HOME

Since silver energy is associated with home, the color props I suggest mainly focus on home furnishings. In my family, silver items were always stored for "something special." Well, now is the time for something special—break out the silver. With this in mind, I think it's helpful to create a sacred silver corner of your home, a kind of intentional area where you can physically activate silver to honor it.

Select an area where you can connect with silver energy. It could be a yoga or stretching space, a meditation nook, or any other room. Place a piece of silver in that space where you can physically activate it to remind you of the feminine, homey aspect of your being.

THE SHADOW SIDE OF SILVER

The shadow side of silver primarily is neglecting your home or allowing chaotic energy to persist. It can also show up as being controlling or overprotective of your home space. If you are leaning toward the shadow side of silver, your living situation will feel unkempt, lifeless, or unorganized and in disarray. Someone who is a hoarder usually is an extreme example of imbalanced silver energy. When there is imbalance in our space, it becomes challenging to give and receive energy. Chances are, you are being overprotective with yourself and thus blocking silver energy from flowing. Allow the silver light to help you clear your energy and your space.

CHAPTER 5

❖

BLUE

QUALITIES: Truth and wisdom
SHADOW SIDE: Avoidance; fear or deceit

Working with blue is like taking a shot of energetic truth serum. It provides us with the resolve to speak our mind in an authentic and meaningful way. Blue helps remove any possible denial we may experience when it comes to seeing others for who they really are as opposed to who we want them to be. Blue is one of three primary colors (along with red and yellow) required to create virtually every other color in the spectrum. I find this to be satisfying symbolically, as it is consistent with the qualities that I see in blue. Just as blue must be incorporated as a base in order to create a variety of other colors, a willingness to blend the truth into every situation is a primary ingredient in learning blue's lesson.

In ancient Egypt, the color blue was associated with divinity. The Egyptian god Amun was said to have made his skin blue so he could fly, invisible, through the blue sky and see what people were truly up to. The Hindu god Vishnu, who appears strikingly blue in artwork, was said to be preserver of the world and possessed the power to know about all beings simultaneously.

In many parts of the world, blue is also thought to protect us against evil. People in Turkey and Greece wear a blue *nazar*—an eye-shaped charm, representing the eye of God— to ward off the "evil eye" from those who wish us harm. In the Middle East, a *hamsa*—a hand-shaped amulet with a blue eye in the center—is often hung in homes to protect against the jealousy of others. This is relevant because jealousy and envy are often the mind's way of distracting us from facing a truth within ourselves.

Blue is often associated with trustworthiness, which could be the reason why many law-enforcement agencies use blue for their uniforms. In this context, blue is used to symbolize a feeling of good faith. Blue is the color of the daytime sky and the ocean, so it is naturally one of the most prevalent colors we see anytime we step outside or are near a body of water. I find this to be meaningful, as the color of truth and wisdom literally blankets the earth in such natural abundance. And on the topic of symbols, what is a more profound symbol of truth than the fidelity of marriage? We take vows with the intention to "be true" to each other. Brides often wear something blue (along with something old, something new, and something borrowed) as a traditional sign of loyalty.

When we come to the planet, I believe we are meant to learn certain fundamental truths. Gratitude, strength, compassion, and compromise are just a few of the life lessons that we may be challenged to learn. However, we have control over the day-to-day decisions that determine our specific path toward acquiring this wisdom. This is why free will exists. We must make our own choices (and mistakes) so that we are given the opportunity to evolve.

No matter what plan or goals we set for our lives, every decision we make guides us toward learning our own series of personal truths. In my view, this is why we may experience pain or loss at certain points in our lives. Those moments help clarify the element of truth and provide us insight that we need to move forward. The honesty of blue lifts the veil from our consciousness and reveals the truths of the universe.

I have a very special relationship with the color blue, as it prompted me to come out of the closet and tell my family that I am gay. I first began studying color energy at the age of 15, and once I reached blue, I was flooded with a desire for honesty in all areas of my life. Blue helped me realize I could not live a truly authentic life without embracing the truth of my sexuality. I grew up in a conservative town, and, like many gay kids, I was hesitant to own my truth for fear of rejection by my family and community. Living in the shadow side of blue caused several adverse effects in my life.

I had been giving readings professionally from the age of 18 and doing a decent job, but harboring this secret was blocking me from accessing deeper insight for others. Avoiding our personal truth causes shame that can lead to a variety of other issues. Aside from affecting my readings negatively, my avoidance of the truth caused me to use emotional eating to fill the emptiness it created.

We are all looking for answers in life, to understand why we are gifted with some situations and then challenged by others. Almost everyone has a "why me?" moment when struggling with a personal issue. Although I know it is a blessing now, being gay was a challenge early in my life. Some of the kids in my school used derogatory gay slurs, and it scared me. I knew the reality that not everyone would connect with my vulnerable honesty, particularly if it conflicted with their religious beliefs. It can also take time to understand that other people's judgment often says more about them than it does about you, especially if they themselves are in denial about something.

I continued my search for answers, and this included activating blue light. I was enamored with healing crystals at the
time and carried a small bag of gemstones around my neck
every day for weeks or months at a time. For many of us on
a spiritual journey, healing stones awaken us to the power of
physical activation. When I decided to come out of the closet
at the age of 19, I first told my family and circle of friends.
And the truth is, some of my loved ones did have objections
to my being openly gay. Not everyone accepted that truth,
and some people in my life really struggled with it. However,
any rejection others may have felt toward me was really none
of my business. Instead, the depth, power, and love I felt from
my core supportive soul group members far outweighed any
rejection I have ever experienced.

Once I acknowledged this truth to my loved ones, a
variety of blessings came rushing into my life. I established
a much closer relationship with my family. The emptiness
inside of me was instead filled with love, and I lost about 80
pounds within the year. It was as though a literal weight was
lifted off my shoulders. This newfound freedom also cleared
my intuitive abilities, for seeing our own truth makes it that
much easier to see it in others. Blue freed me to come from a
truly authentic place of loving guidance. To me, it felt like the
world had finally opened up. While my personal journey and
experience may be different from yours, we can all benefit
from a boost of truthful blue energy in our lives.

As an intuitive life coach, I am honored to regularly take
a glimpse into the life journeys of people all over the world,
and I use blue to help facilitate this process. I do this by stepping into the energy of the person I am working with. When
I am asked for guidance on a life decision, for example, the
first thing that I do is see how truthful that decision feels
within their energy. If it is in their best interest, the energy

will expand and feel good. If it is not the best choice, it will just feel wrong and the energy will contract. Blue increases my ability to speak the truth no matter what the client may want to hear.

One of the things I love most about my work is how much I learn from my clients in the process. I believe every soul on this planet has their own wisdom to offer, their own unique perspective, and their own obstacles to recognizing that wisdom. Part of the challenge is in understanding why we are here and what the blocks we need to overcome are. Blue reminds us not to feel daunted if there are a lot of life issues that need to be dealt with. That is the whole point of our journey through life! There is an element of truth in every situation that must be accepted before we can evolve or change in any way, and this is not always easy for us to do. Blue gives us the strength to tune in to our inherent wisdom and truth, even if that truth is painful.

One of my clients, Erica, used blue energy to help her with a major phobia. She was agoraphobic, having a fear of public spaces. It had gotten so bad that Erica only left her apartment to go food shopping once a month. And with the advent of online grocery delivery, even that outing was at risk of being eliminated. Erica's mother, a client of mine, had gifted her daughter with a coaching package for her birthday. We began working together over the phone, and I suggested blue as a tool to help give her the courage to face her situation.

I also asked her, in addition to activating blue, to try a "worst-case scenario" exercise (outlined below in the spiritual activation notes). Erica wanted to overcome her fear of public spaces but felt like it was out of her control. She knew logically that nothing bad would happen by going out in public. But the pattern of staying within the safety of her home perpetuated her irrational fear. Together, we decided that the best way to proceed would be to invite members of her soul group to help out.

As part of the exercise, Erica contacted her older sister, Julie, with whom she was very close. Her sister suggested they meet at a coffee shop, but only for five minutes, which Erica immediately dismissed as too far outside of her comfort zone. Julie then suggested they make a weekly date to see each other at Erica's apartment. After doing this for a month successfully, Erica agreed to sit on a park bench outside her building for five minutes. It was not easy for her, but every few weeks, they continued trying something new.

Activating blue also helped Erica finally admit to her sister and to me that she had secretly stopped taking her anxiety medication. Although it had been working, Erica felt that taking medication was a failure to overcome this issue on her own, so she made the decision to stop. While I think that medication should be a last resort, I completely support it as part of a whole-body approach to overall health. Far too many people who suffer from depression think they should be able to deal with it on their own. We would never question the need for insulin or heart medication, so why do we treat depression any differently? Addressing our mental health is something to be proud of, as it means we are taking care of ourselves.

After a few months, Erica felt strong enough to meet an old friend for a meal. This was an ongoing process, but she now makes sure to leave her apartment at least once a day as part of her self-care. I don't mean to make it sound like blue was some kind of magic pill. She did the work. But activating blue served as a useful tool to show her when to ask for help.

ACTIVATING BLUE NOTES

AM I BEING COMPLETELY HONEST WITH MYSELF?

Blue is what I would describe as a "prickly" color for some people to activate. If I tell a client that I'm about to say something prickly, it means they may not like what they are about to hear. But the message is intended to help them learn the lesson of a situation so they can move forward. Since blue is the color of truth and wisdom, it will open your eyes to areas of your life that need attention. This may bring up difficult feelings if you don't want to accept the truth, but that is where the wisdom part comes in. Using blue brings you the courage to see things clearly and the wisdom to release your attachment to the illusion that truth reveals. I encourage you to experiment with it and see what comes up for you.

Oftentimes in life, we become so immersed in our daily routine that we forget whether or not we are being true to ourselves and actually aligned with the life we want. This can occur in any area, but nowhere is this more apparent than in relationships. Most of us spend our lives searching for a soul group that makes us feel safe. But then, once we are lucky enough to find them, we sometimes forget to be our true selves. No one intends for this to happen, but if we are not careful, little by little, we begin to hold back from expressing our true feelings. This is usually because we don't want to be misunderstood and would like to avoid potential conflict, but there is also another reason. True honesty requires us to be vulnerable, and sometimes it is just easier to bottle up that blue energy at the end of a long day.

Countless issues would be healed if we could let our guard down and allow the truth to be reflected back to us. Perhaps your partner feels insecure, neglected, or misunderstood, and they need to express this. But what tends to happen is that the shadow side of blue prevents us from hearing that truth, and instead we become defensive. Rather than receiving the underlying truth of the message, we hear it as criticism. If you have ever had a difficult but honest conversation with a loved one that resulted in mutual understanding and resolution, you know the feeling of balanced blue energy.

Blue has the power to enable real change in your life. Allow it to show you that you are strong enough to accept any difficult truths and move past them.

SPIRITUAL ACTIVATION NOTES

Fear is a completely natural part of human nature. Its purpose is to protect us from harming ourselves (keeping us from things such as touching a hot stove or crossing the street before looking both ways). However, unchecked fear can hold us back from stepping out of our comfort zone and pursuing our passion. Spiritual activation can be a powerful way to release us from the grip of fear and transform it into truthful abundance.

SPIRITUAL ACTIVATION EXERCISE: THE WORST-CASE SCENARIO

This exercise is useful for shining light on a fear that is keeping you from enjoying your life. Fear does not have to be a full-blown phobia. Any kind of irrational hesitation that keeps you from moving forward is worth examining. Fear can continue to persist after you acknowledge it, so it may require additional steps to recondition yourself to step past it.

1. After spiritually activating blue through meditation, take a piece of paper and ask yourself the following question: *What is the worst thing that could happen if I do the thing that I am afraid of?* Go ahead and write down everything that comes up, regardless of how irrational the fear may seem. The answer may come to you immediately or it may take some time to surface. Either way, intend to use the blue light as a tool for your honest acceptance of the truth.

2. Reach out to at least one member of your soul group and ask for their help and support. Tell them about your fear and see if they have any ideas that might be helpful.

3. Outline at least one step that you can take every day toward accepting and moving past this fear. Ask your loved one to help you by accompanying you in confronting this fear. Having them follow up will hold you accountable to your plan.

It's important to remember everyone experiences fear in their own way. Even the most accomplished people you look up to have at some point been faced with an opportunity that truly scares them. But courageous people acknowledge the fear and then go ahead and take that opportunity anyway. Many people assume that living your truth requires monumental changes in lifestyle. But in my opinion, it's better to take baby steps that create lasting change than to be overwhelmed by the prospect of a major change and do nothing at all.

Examples of confronting common fears are:

- Going out for a meal or a movie alone.

- Setting up an online dating profile. This means using a current picture and making an honest effort at creating a positive description of yourself.

- Starting a new health regimen.

- Overcoming the fear of public speaking. This could include making a toast at a wedding.

Once you have decided on a fear to confront, it is critical to declare your intention to a loved one. Allow yourself to ask for help and receive support. Try to release any shame, as enabling this kind of growth is the universe's intended purpose for your soul group. Finally, follow up with your group or a loved one to talk about the feelings or shift in energy you had as you faced your fear. The purpose of blue is to face your truth with courage, and I know you can do it!

UNIVERSAL ACTIVATION NOTES (AKA "I SPY" WITH MY INTUITIVE EYE)

Blue is one of the easiest colors for universal activation. All you have to do is look up at the sky to be reminded of truthful blue. Whenever you see and notice blue, remember what it means for your energy and ask yourself the following questions: Am I being honest with myself? Am I avoiding the reality of some situation? In lieu of an activation exercise, here is an in-depth example of how a client experienced a powerful transformation with blue.

I was in New York City on business, and Linda came to me for an intuitive reading. Most new clients are a bit nervous at first, as they are not sure what to expect. Some people are fearful I am going to read their thoughts. Let me reassure you—I am not a mind reader. What I look at are the overall elements of your life swirling around in your aura.

Linda had shoulder-length wavy brown hair and was in her midthirties. She sat down on the upholstered couch, with a view of Central Park behind her, and smiled nervously. As soon as I focused on her, all I could see in my mind's eye was a library full of blue books. When I begin a psychic reading, I often start to see symbolic images in my mind. It is an experience I refer to as "cosmic charades."

Cosmic charades is the universe's way of presenting me with information about my client through images that are familiar to my life. If I am with a client and I suddenly see my father, who works in real estate, then I will ask my client if they also work in real estate. In Linda's case, I saw a library, which to me shows a strong desire for knowledge. Another intuitive might see something else that represents knowledge to them; perhaps their spouse would pop into their head if that person was extremely honest. It all depends on what image the universe thinks will get the message across.

As I focused on Linda's energy, I saw more and more of this blue library scene. Moonlight was shining through the windows and showering the books with every shade of blue possible. For me, a library and the books in it represent not only knowledge but also a profound need for answers. In many cases, a person is craving truth because they feel someone is deceiving them. Some of my colleagues have speculated this visual might be my version of a person's Akashic records.

"Linda, we haven't even started the session, and yet I am very aware of the presence of blue energy around you. Blue is the color of truth and wisdom. It also teaches us about fear and avoidance. Part of what we are going to discuss today will be the areas of your life where you aren't living your truth. It seems like fear might be causing you to hesitate from revealing your true being in certain areas."

Linda stared at me for a moment, then burst out laughing. "You just get right to the point, don't you?"

We both shared a laugh, and I proceeded.

When I see blue in a client's aura, it tends to be incredibly rich and varied. Much like the colors of the ocean, there are many shades and hues of blue, depending on where you look. There is a richness to blue that envelops the room. Typically, it is seen around someone who wants to research, study, and understand every aspect of life. People with blue energy are seekers of truth. And yet, if there is a strong presence of very *dark* blue in their aura, I often find they have trouble accepting their own truth. They may be suspicious of people in their circle for a variety of reasons.

"Linda, your trust issues feel like they are through the roof right now. It's like you question everyone's intentions and have trouble accepting anyone's word at face value. Why is that?"

Linda turned red. "I have been cheated on before."

"But this feels like it's currently happening."

"Well, I am dating a guy now."

When I am doing a psychic reading, cosmic charades makes me feel as if the universe is jumping around my client, trying to get me to guess what is going on in their life. It's almost as if the universe is visually pantomiming the message I need to convey. With Linda, my glimpse into her life was through this library full of blue books. I could only tell that she struggled with trust and was seeking truth, but I didn't know why. I waited for another visual to present itself to me.

"What's your boyfriend's name?" I asked.

"Jim."

The moment she uttered his name, I saw a volcanic explosion in my mind. The erupting volcano was another clue from the universe, which told me her relationship was extremely passionate and slightly dangerous. She enjoyed their fiery chemistry, but it would eventually burn out, and Linda might get hurt in the process.

"Linda, I see a lot of passion between you and Jim. But, to be honest, it does not feel safe to me."

Linda had met Jim at the investment bank where they worked and had been seeing him for over a year. They had incredibly passionate chemistry. She loved Jim, but there was a problem. He was married.

"I hate to say this, Linda, but I do not see him leaving his wife for you."

"You sound just like my friends. But he is already separated from his wife and is planning to divorce her."

Saying I felt unsafe about her new boyfriend might sound like a simple and generic statement, but to an intuitive, it means a lot. When I am tuning in to a client, I am literally "trying on" their energy to see how their life path feels to me. If they ask me about any life situation, I check how this energy makes me feel inside before responding.

There are a variety of things I may or may not see in a client's energy. If there is new love, I will sometimes see fireworks in the night sky. Fireworks symbolize passion, but they explode in the distance, where you can enjoy their thrill safely. A volcano also erupts spectacularly, but it spews burning lava that destroys everything in its path. Even though these kinds of images symbolize passion, they are also signs of the early, short-term stages of a relationship. To me, true and lasting love feels sensual yet safe, like cuddling under a warm cashmere blanket in front of a fireplace, watching snow fall outside. On the other end of the spectrum, if a client is struggling through a troubled relationship, I feel anxious, cold, or stressed. I might see myself locked out of a house in the freezing rain without an umbrella. With Linda and Jim, I felt major heat, but the energy wasn't flowing evenly between them. Most importantly, I felt unsafe.

"So, Linda, how do you feel about Jim?"

"I love him. I just wish that he would get divorced so we can be together for real."

"Are you okay with things staying the way that they are?"

"No. I want to get married and have kids one day."

"Have you given him any kind of time limit for how long you will wait until he divorces his wife?"

"Not exactly."

She spent the next portion of her session talking about her hopes for their future. As Linda kept talking, it was painfully obvious that Jim was in no hurry at all to marry her. It was like watching the volcano destroy an entire village. Jim and his wife still owned an apartment together on the Upper West Side, and he stayed with her several nights a week. I think Linda knew the truth on some level but was not ready to admit it to herself. This was a perfect example of blue's shadow side. Linda's energy was full of shadowy blue because she did not want to face a truth in her life. She needed honesty in her relationship but was also afraid of receiving the true answer. My gut feeling was she picked a married man because she was subconsciously afraid of being cheated on again. It was easier to be with someone that was unavailable right from the start.

"Linda, in order to create trust and emotional depth in a relationship, we have to let people in. You are blocking the natural progression of this relationship by not expressing your truth to Jim. It is certainly possible he will leave his wife for you, but you are not truly owning this as a possibility."

She frowned and looked annoyed. "I don't understand."

"Linda, if someone asked you out on a date today, what would you say?"

"I would tell them that I'm in a relationship."

"Exactly. Jim is holding the space of your life partner, even though he is not able to fill that role for you. Now, this may be hard to hear, but I think you are subconsciously blocking blue energy. Do me a favor. Close your eyes, and I want you to envision yourself surrounded by the radiant blue light of truth. Take a few deep breaths in through your nose and out through your mouth. The truth is what it is, and we can only gain by bearing witness to it. No one is here but us. When you are ready, I have a question that I want you to answer truthfully. Don't hesitate and don't filter yourself."

Linda exhaled deeply and nodded. "Okay."

"If he is going to divorce his wife, why hasn't he done it yet?"

"Because it's easier for him not to. He gets the best of both worlds."

"And why haven't you given him an ultimatum?"

She opened her eyes and they began welling up with tears. "I don't want to be alone."

As Oprah would say, this was our aha moment, brought about by blue energy. In life, so many of us are afraid to express our truth. We fear being hurt, and so we create scenarios to help us avoid it. In this case, Linda's brain was telling her that she should stay quiet and compromise so she wouldn't have to be alone. But really, she picked Jim to protect herself from being cheated on again.

"Linda, you deserve to have what you want. Jim is not being completely fair with you. He is holding space in your life as a partner but is currently unable to truly stand by your side. I think what we are dealing with here is taking a risk and expressing your truth. And when we do that, we create a sense of vulnerability, which, of course, is scary."

Our future is never written in stone; only the lessons we are meant to learn are. When I am tuning in to a client, my intention is to help them step through the lesson at hand and move forward. Linda needed to learn how to trust again. She wanted to be with Jim, so I counseled her to give him a chance to be the man she wanted him to be. She had to take a stand in order for the relationship to take its intended course, good or bad. But ultimately, she was in control of how this would play out. I just wanted her to feel strong enough to see the truth of their relationship, no matter what it was.

"Linda, I feel that you are working on attracting your soul mate, and the only way we can find out if Jim is your soul mate is by giving him the chance to come through for you. You need to express your truth to him and tell him what you need for this relationship to work."

When Linda left that day, she was not happy with the reading, and I don't blame her. I did not tell her what she wanted to hear. But my job is to counsel people on the work they need to do in order to move forward, not necessarily to make them feel good. My parting advice to Linda was to try activating blue light regularly, because I thought it could help her get the resolution that she needed.

About eight months later, Linda e-mailed me. She had indeed been unhappy with the reading at the time, but what I said about blue had stuck in her mind. Anytime she looked up at the sky, she was reminded of our session and what I had said about her needing to face the truth. One day, something clicked. She finally gave Jim an ultimatum and a firm calendar date by which he had to decide. The date passed and, sure enough, he admitted he was not divorcing his wife. While hurt by the breakup, Linda was ultimately happy with her decision. She had started therapy and finally acknowledged she was subconsciously attracted to unavailable partners so she wouldn't have to face being hurt again. Linda closed the e-mail by saying that not long after this, she met a nice new guy and had been dating him for a month. And this time, he was single for real.

I think Linda's experience resonates with so many of us. We hesitate to express our truth for fear of experiencing pain. But bright blue freedom is waiting on the other side of that pain. What I love about the energy of blue is that it holds the potential to catapult us forward. In a perfect world, Jim would have swept Linda into his arms after she expressed her truth. He would have finally divorced his wife, married Linda, and lived happily ever after. But Jim's purpose was to teach Linda the lesson of trust, not to be her soul mate. Even though activating blue brought her some short-term pain, the truth moved her on to a man that was truly available for the depth, commitment, and passion she was looking for.

BLUE AFFIRMATION

I HAVE THE STRENGTH TO SEE THE TRUTH.

PHYSICAL ACTIVATION NOTES

When I speak at a live event, I often wear blue as it reminds me of my intention to be a conduit of truthful guidance. It is one of my favorite colors to activate during sessions. I have some blue accent pillows in my office as a visual reminder to speak only truth to those that seek my counsel. I am a people pleaser and want everyone to be happy, but my job is to provide truthful guidance. Blue energy empowers me to do that.

Some blue color props you could incorporate into your day include:

- **Blueberries.** Yes, you can use food as a physical activation! The bounty of natural produce is a beautiful way for your body to literally absorb the power of color.

- **Blue quartz crystals.** These lovely crystals are a perfect color prop to help you find the truth in any situation.

- **Blue dress shirt.** A classic and easy way to incorporate blue is through clothing such as a shirt or blouse.

PHYSICAL ACTIVATION EXERCISE: EXPRESS YOUR TRUTH

This exercise will help you receive the strength to see the truth of a situation. Before you begin, find a quiet space where you will not be disturbed for at least 15 minutes. The goal here is to make you more comfortable with seeing things as they really are. You will be meditating on a series of questions as you visualize blue.

1. Select a color prop to use for this exercise.

2. Once you have your color prop nearby, write down this question: *Where am I not living my truth?*

3. Put your pen down, hold your color prop in your hands, and close your eyes. If you like, you

can set a timer for five minutes. (I find that this helps to quiet a busy mind for a few moments.) With the question clearly in your consciousness, continue touching the color prop and take deliberate, slow, deep breaths. With each inhalation, imagine the blue energy of the color prop entering your body through your hands, and filling you up. This blue energy is helping your higher self receive truthful and honest answers to your question. What you are looking for here is honest feedback from your higher self on where you are *not* living your truth.

4. Keep touching your color prop as you intend to receive the answer that your higher self wants to give you. Do not worry if what comes up is painful or difficult to hear; just try to listen without judgment. You have nothing to prove to anyone.

5. When you feel ready, or when your timer goes off, open your eyes and write down the answer that comes to your mind. Try not to judge the answer, just write down the thoughts that come to you. This can be a few lines or several pages. It all depends on what comes to you.

6. Think of at least one actionable step you can take to honor your truth. Do not worry if this step feels difficult to carry out in the moment. Fear has a way of finding excuses for us not to change, but that is not the point. The important thing is to *acknowledge* the truth of what needs to be done. By activating blue, your higher self will bring you closer to the answer.

There are so many ways we can ignore our truths. This is where the power of blue will shine for you; it invokes the courage to be who you are.

THE SHADOW SIDE OF BLUE

If blue represents truth and wisdom, then the shadow side of blue is fear of that truth. An imbalance of blue typically manifests as a refusal to accept the reality of a situation, but it can also show up as deception (either being deceived or doing the deceiving). That uneasy feeling that someone is lying to us, or the guilt we feel when lying to someone else, is a classic sign of a blue imbalance. No matter the situation, the shadow side of blue is a struggle when it comes to facing the truth of a situation. Activating blue will bring out the truth, but if this area is out of balance, it will also highlight how fear plays a role in our life. This is why blue can be "prickly" for people to activate, though it gives us the power to unlock our cage of denial and soar into the exhilarating freedom of truth.

Many of us waste precious time ignoring or running away from aspects of ourselves that we struggle to accept. While I completely understand the desire to avoid a difficult truth, this prevents us from learning its lesson and moving past our fear. The irony of blue's shadow side is that no one can avoid the truth forever. Staying in an unhealthy relationship or denying the existence of an addiction may seem easier in the short term, but this just causes blue's imbalance to grow until our lives are dwarfed by its massive shadow. If we continue clinging to the shadow side of blue, the imbalance can even begin to manifest in health issues. At some point, we will be forced to acknowledge the lesson.

The whole point of living is to learn a series of lessons so that we can evolve, and blue will shine a light on those lessons. Human beings naturally want to avoid feeling pain, but every one of us will at some point be faced with a situation too painful not to deal with. I just want to reassure you that a beautiful bright blue freedom waits on the other side of that truth.

We live in an era of unprecedented opportunity to find and express our truth (to varying degrees, depending on where you live in the world). This is especially true due to developments in technology. The Internet offers unlimited access to information, and we know that truth is the embodiment of blue energy. We do not have to rely on others to learn about any given topic. We are free to become as informed as we wish to be.

Social media has become a platform for every person with an Internet connection who wishes to share their thoughts and feelings on any given topic. In the past, only celebrities and politicians had this kind of opportunity to express themselves openly to the world. We can now express our truth and receive support from kindred spirits far beyond our physical community. In addition, disenfranchised minorities and those affected by social injustice of all kinds have been given a powerful voice and audience. If you are activating blue and want to feel the instant effects of speaking your truth, social media is truly a modern miracle.

And yet how truthful are we really? These days, it is common to keep up with friends by posting a recent photo of ourselves on various social media platforms. This practice is so common that high school reunions have been basically rendered obsolete, due to the fact we can connect with and follow up with literally anyone we have ever known. And just like at a high school reunion, it is natural to want to present the best possible version of ourselves to our peers.

Many people go to great lengths to make sure their lives look as perfect as possible online. Before posting a photo, we might get dressed up, put on makeup, fix our hair, find nice lighting, and take a variety of photos at flattering angles until we find one that looks just right. Then we will edit out any blemishes using an app on our phone and make sure that our skin glows. The end result is the same as if a professional photographer came to take our picture for a magazine! While nothing is inherently wrong with wanting to look our best, taking this process too far feeds into the shadow side of blue by promoting unrealistic expectations. It is not exactly the truth, but rather some curated approximation of it.

We all naturally want to project the ideal version of our lives to the world. But if we are not mindful, we may end up entirely concealing our truth under a flattering filter. Scrolling through posts of models and pop stars lounging on yachts may seem harmless, but we often end up feeling bad when we compare our lives to their seemingly glamorous ones. What we don't see behind that reality TV star's flawless makeup selfie is the eating disorder, the chronic depression, the abusive relationship, or whatever else they don't want you to notice. This is the double-edged sword of social media. Truth and lies are two sides of the same blue coin.

I have received the following message in meditation so many times, and my hope is for you to ingest the truth of it: you are perfect exactly as you are.

Any struggles you currently face are just lessons the universe wants you to learn. You will learn these lessons sooner or later; blue energy just speeds up that process. Blue teaches us to go beneath our surface, to dig up the weeds of denial. Once we do this, the truth nourishes our spiritual garden and allows flowers of wisdom to flourish.

CHAPTER 6

❖

EMERALD GREEN

QUALITIES: Communication and creativity
SHADOW SIDE: Blocked self-expression

Emerald green helps us open our lines of creativity and communication. While there are many shades of green, I find that the deeper shades, like emerald, are best for when you want to let your creative juices flow. On the communication front, emerald will help clear misunderstandings in your relationships and allow you to find the perfect words to express yourself.

Culturally, green is often associated with the freedom to move forward and flourish. A green traffic light is internationally recognized as the sign to "go ahead," while a green card grants permanent residence in the United States. Having a green thumb indicates a natural ability to make plants grow. This coincides nicely with the way I view creativity, which is that we essentially use our hands to create. In the science world, green is considered a relaxing color for the eye to take in, and studies have shown that being around emerald green can also reduce fatigue.[1]

Emerald green helps us to connect with the creative or artistic aspect of ourselves. In my practice, I usually see emerald around singers, public speakers, and writers or artisans.

Maya Angelou, the prolific poet, and pop artist Andy Warhol are perfect examples of creative emerald green energy.

When using green, it is important to channel this powerful energy by highlighting the artist within you. This color will stimulate a desire to create from the soul, and that process is not complete until we have a tangible expression of our creativity. For many of us, this simply involves getting out of our own way and allowing the artist within us to create. We all have a creative side, regardless of what we may tell ourselves. And just because you may not make your living as an artist does not mean you have no creativity to express. If you have ever enjoyed writing poetry, painting, dancing, photography, or even just putting together an outfit to wear for the day, then you are connecting with a source of dark green energy within you. Emerald will help you revitalize and bring out that expression of creativity in yourself.

Green's creativity-enhancing effects have been shown through a wealth of scientific evidence. Stephanie Lichtenfeld, a psychologist with the University of Munich, conducted a series of experiments to test the psychological effects of the color green.[2] In one experiment, 69 participants were given two minutes to come up with as many uses as possible for a tin can. Before starting the task, half of the students looked at a computer screen showing green, while the other half observed a computer screen showing white. The goal was to see how subjects' brainstorming abilities were affected by the use of color. Upon completing the test, participants who looked at green scored about 20 percent higher. The lesson here is that creativity does not only refer to traditional hobbies like painting. You can use green to stimulate possibilities and solutions that might not otherwise come to you as easily.

In a different experiment, 35 German college students were asked to look at a geometric figure and then draw as many geometric objects as they could in two and a half minutes. Just as in the previous study, this experiment tested how the color green would affect brainstorming abilities. However, in this case subjects were using the visual medium of drawing instead of working with ideas. Before beginning this exercise, half the participants looked at a green image, while the other half looked at a gray image. The students who looked at green were found to be more creative, drawing more geometric objects than those who looked at gray.

Another experiment was conducted in the series, this time using high school students. But in this case, students were shown green, blue, or red before beginning the exercise. The goal was to see if *any* color could stimulate creativity or if it was specific colors. In this case, the students who were exposed to green exhibited higher levels of creativity than those who were exposed to red or blue. What I love about these kinds of findings is they show the variety of ways in which green can be used. Creativity is a quality that can be utilized visually, conceptually, through sound, and in myriad other areas. Working with green, even briefly, will give you a valuable boost of creativity you can use wherever you like!

One of the questions I am sometimes asked about working with color energy involves making sure it is exactly the right shade (in this case, emerald green). You may be concerned you are perhaps using the wrong *shade* of green, and that it will not be effective for you if this is the case. While I completely understand the desire for accuracy, let me put you at ease. I'd like to clarify that you do not have to see the exact emerald shade of green in order to spark creativity in your life. When I see emerald green around people, I am referring to any medium to deep shade of green. Remember, this is not an exact science. Basically, as long as you are in the general vicinity of the color (as in, any kind of deeper green), you are on the right track.

Here is another experiment to support the idea that you don't need an exact shade of green in order to benefit from using the color. In a study in the United Kingdom, 108 students were split into three groups and tested to see the creative effects of the color green. The first group of students used green paper to take a creativity test. The second group was tested in a classroom that was filled with green plants and had windows with views of natural scenery. Finally, the third group took the test in a classroom that had no exposure to the color green. The results showed that being exposed to green made both the first and second sets of students more visually creative than the students who saw no green. But the most fascinating element of this study was that students who used green paper were *just as* creative as the students who were around real plants and saw views of nature.[3]

The green paper in this experiment was not the exact same shade as that of the live plants and nature, yet it had the same effect for the students. Of course, it would be ideal (for a variety of reasons) to go outside and absorb green energy by looking at plants and nature directly. But you can still benefit from green even if you don't have access to a natural setting in your daily life. Seeing the color green, *in any form*, will give you a boost of its creative energy. For an immediate boost of creativity, try setting your computer background to an image of something green! That's what I like to do when I am writing or taking on any kind of creative endeavor that involves my computer.

Another welcome effect of emerald green is, it helps us reduce stress and feel relaxed. While being calm is not a requirement for creativity, I personally find I am much more able to express myself creatively when I feel loose and decompressed. Supportive of this idea is a stress study at VU University Medical Center in Amsterdam. Around four dozen college students took a computerized math test and were simultaneously monitored with sensors that detected their hearts' electrical activity. During the increasingly difficult math exam, the students were shown on-screen comparisons of their results with much higher national averages. Perhaps it is due to the fact that math has never been my strong suit, but this test sounds like a nightmare to me! In any case, all the students were given failing grades, regardless of their actual results.

Why were all the students made to fail? The study was measuring the effect of green on students' stress, and failing a hard exam is a good way of achieving the goal of being stressed! This test was chosen for its proven history of raising stress levels for students. The only difference between the two groups of students was that half of them viewed green images before and after taking the test, while the other half viewed images that did not contain any green. And wouldn't you know it, the students who viewed the green images had significantly lower heart rates after the stressful test. According to Magdalena van den Berg, who led the study, "short durations of viewing green pictures may help people to recover from stress."[4]

Pablo Picasso is reported to have said, "Every child is an artist. The problem is staying an artist when you grow up." I love that quote, and I think it speaks strongly to the challenge we all face in fostering creativity throughout our lives. Children love to dress up in costume, dance, sing, and use their imaginations freely. As adults, however, we often forget about expressing ourselves, and we focus instead on the to-do list of our lives. Not only that, but there is also the mistaken belief that no one but professional artists has the right to showcase their creativity. Self-expression may not seem important to you, but living with this kind of unexpressed, stagnant energy is one of the most common reasons my clients feel an imbalance in their lives. Utilizing your originality transcends hobbies like art and will overflow into other areas of your life, with wonderful results. This is also why emerald—or deep, rich green—is about to become such a powerful addition to your creative toolbox.

I believe an artist exists in all of us. Part of our soul's desire is to express itself, and creativity is the lifeblood of self-expression. Any person who invokes their inner artist is immediately surrounded by swirls of green energy. For some, being artistic may be an easy energy to access. Or perhaps your creative side isn't as obvious. I will explain my creative journey with green below, but the main thing you should know about this color is it is even *more* important if you do not see yourself as creative or particularly expressive. Even if you are a financial advisor, attorney, or someone who might not traditionally see themselves as creative, emerald green can be used to solve difficult problems and arrive at new potential solutions to any situation. That is the point of strengthening this energy. It will open new avenues of creative possibility and bring a sense of calm balance to your life.

Be patient with your personal exploration of creativity. For some reason, artistic expression has the power to inspire self-criticism in some. This feeling can be reduced when we find an outlet that makes our soul sing.

Allow yourself the freedom to experiment with different forms of creative expression and see how each one makes you feel. As you begin to invoke your creative self, emerald green energy will help you move into a variety of creative expressions. It is easy to identify creativity with painting, dancing, music, sculpture, drawing, or some of the more traditional forms of creative expression. Or perhaps your creativity manifests in writing, as it does for me. The point is, it doesn't matter how you express yourself, as long as you do it.

When we activate emerald green, we are invoking the energy of communication. This applies not only to artistic expression, but to verbal expression as well. Darker green highlights the way our words, thoughts, and intentions flow from us. Using this color will affect the way our expression is received within our community and, more importantly, what energy will be brought into our lives in return. An added benefit of working with this color is it will help you to express yourself with other people in a fundamental way.

Our feelings sometimes get stifled somewhere between our hearts and our mouths. Yet conveying our feelings accurately through words is a critical part of any healthy relationship. Countless relationships are needlessly put at risk by the trap of thinking, *I don't have to say how I feel; she already knows.* Our actions are equally as important as the words we use with loved ones. We were blessed with a voice that allows us to relate to other people. Green can help us find the words we need to express how we really feel.

Communication is such a powerful tool, because it allows us to connect with other people and hopefully overcome differences of opinion. In today's charged climate, our world is often inundated with nasty fights and hostile opposition to any different idea. Turn on a political news show at any time and you will see examples of this. We often disagree over religious and political beliefs, which is what creates separation in the world. This separation allows us to believe we are somehow morally better than those who hold different views.

However, we often find common ground more easily when it comes to artistic expression. Art can cross religious as well as political divides. Creativity has the power to make us feel alive and ask questions.

The suggestions I make to my clients are ideas that I intuitively believe are in alignment with their unique personal expression, but it is up to them to take the steps toward realizing that creativity in life. We do not need creativity to live, but it is a critical component to a *happy* life. If we are willing to take real steps toward the creative life that we want, emerald green can and will work its magic.

I have a client (whom I now prefer to call a colleague) who has published several books and utilizes the power of color in various effective ways. She often uses a combination of spiritual, universal, and physical activations to invoke her creative self. I thought it would be fun to interview her on her experience.

INTERVIEW WITH LICIA MORELLI

Dougall: Hi, Licia; thanks for agreeing to share your story. Can you tell me a little bit about your experience with emerald green?

Licia: Of course! I had talked with you about green being really helpful in my process of transition and healing and also in this next phase of my work life. I have taken several classes with you, and green has been my favorite color throughout. It is the color I use during my writing process. I used green for my first book, *Lemonade Hurricane*, which is a children's story that teaches mindfulness and meditation to kids. It is the color I am using to write my next book. I also use green to help me write promotional copy for businesses that need help finding a unique voice. I work with several different businesses, helping them come up with taglines, which has become another way to express my creativity. Green is now the color I invoke as I move forward in my career. It really is one of those colors that changed my life.

Dougall: That's amazing! And if I may ask, how did it change your life?

Licia: Well, you once told me you saw emerald green running down my arms, which indicated that I might be a writer. What you thought was so funny about this was that I never really talked about wanting to be a writer when we first worked together, even though I did. It's just something I omitted from conversations. And what you told me was that I needed to come to a place where I could truly embrace that creative aspect of myself. So green really did change my life. Because for so long, I didn't give myself permission to call myself a writer. I have always loved writing, but I didn't go to school for it. I didn't go to graduate school for an M.F.A. or do any of the things that many authors will have you believe are the steps that you have to take in order to be a legitimate writer.

Dougall: And before we worked together, what was your experience with color in general? You mentioned that green is your favorite. Did you always love green, or did it evolve as a result of us pairing it with the creative intention?

Licia: The intention part of it is something that definitely evolved over time. Because initially, I had no idea about your work with color or what it meant. I think I had heard you on a radio show, and I called in to get a reading. This was before I had taken any kind of classes with you. The first color that you ever saw around me was purple. You talked about how purple is the color of the leader, and that idea really resonated for me at the time. Looking back, I almost see it as there are some colors we easily connect with, and there are other colors we have to graduate into. Purple was a color that came easily for me. I am comfortable being a leader in various parts of my

101

life; I have always helped guide others. Purple felt safe and familiar. But green was a color that was intimidating for me, because it had to do with expressing my personal creativity. I saw green as emotionally exposing myself, because creativity involves putting yourself out there. And it wasn't until you saw green running down my arms that things really clicked for me. You found it remarkable that I was not sharing my creative side with others, when it was clearly such a big part of who I am. And that's when I realized that I wanted to own what I want to say, and own the way I communicate with the world.

Dougall: And the funny thing is, it has always been a huge part of who you are. It was just a matter of putting your creativity at the forefront of your consciousness, as part of your true identity.

Licia: Exactly.

Dougall: And can you tell me a bit about how you use green in your daily life?

Licia: Yes. So when I want to sit down and write, I need to focus. Before I begin writing, I will wear something green or drink out of a green cup. I basically put it in my visual landscape, just to remind me I am working with green. I also feel like green helps me with the emotional aspects of expressing my creativity. Some days, I'll use what I call the "Glinda bubble." I will visualize myself in a big clear bubble, just like Glinda the Good Witch from the movie *The Wizard of Oz*, and then I infuse the bubble with green. I remind myself that the green will be guiding me in the creative decisions I make that day. This energy extends throughout my day, from the e-mails

I write to the social media posts I make. Wherever I communicate with creativity, the green will be infused throughout.

Dougall: And you notice a difference?

Licia: Yes. I more notice that when I'm *not* doing this, it is harder for me to focus on the creative task at hand. Like, instead of writing the book, I'll pick the Internet, or some other thing, to distract myself and avoid my creativity. The green helps me to get into that creative space and stay there.

Dougall: Did you ever notice that green helped bring out an idea for you?

Licia: It was more that it helped me with writer's block. One of the things I sometimes struggle with is taking one of my blog posts and then fleshing it out from a few paragraphs into a whole chapter. If I ever felt blocked, I would visualize emerald green running down my arms, through my fingertips, and into the keyboard. I'd see the keyboard light up in green from the energy flowing through my arms, and then things would just start coming to me. It's like the green energy lent stamina to my efforts.

Dougall: Amazing. Thank you so much, Licia!

ACTIVATING EMERALD GREEN NOTES

WHERE AM I EXPRESSING MY CREATIVITY?

Communication and creativity go hand in hand. How often do we have the room to express who we are from a soul level? Most working adults spend the majority of their day aligning with the expression of another person in their job. Your job may be to highlight the company brand, or perhaps you teach someone else's curriculum. The examples of putting someone else first are limitless in most people's lives. But in the art world, we are given the opportunity to find our own voice and our own point of view. As we activate emerald green, we reconnect with our voice. We shine a light on our own unique spark of life and create a safe environment to express our true feelings and core.

Self-expression does not only mean you are personally creating some kind of "art." A great way to support this energy in your life is to appreciate the music, acting, or photography of other artists. You can use this energy to awaken your own creativity. For example, if I write a new blog, I need to use an image that will accompany the piece. I will often visit websites that support independent, lesser-known photographers and graphic designers. I can spend hours searching for the perfect image to echo the message of my blog. I love the idea that, somewhere in the world, another person is accessing their creative spirit. That creative expression then joins with my writing to invoke a well-rounded, meaningful message. I may not have taken the photo, but I connect to my own creativity simply by appreciating the work of another artist.

Deep, rich emerald green tends to move quickly for people, meaning you will notice its effects almost immediately as you work with it. The reason for this is that when creativity is flowing properly, you do not censor or think too much. Ideas or possibilities may come to you, and your job is to allow them to manifest physically. Try not to restrain your initial creative urges, as this will only stifle the energy of emerald green. It is always easier to edit your personal expression later than it is to release it in the first place. The best way to utilize this color is to allow it to flow and inspire you with whatever you are doing.

The idea is to color outside the lines. If you lean toward following rules in your life, you may be slightly apprehensive with green. This is completely normal. Emerald green helps to foster a sense of freedom, but the flip side of this excitement is apprehension. If you are naturally a person that marches to the beat of your own drum, then green will probably flow through your being quite easily.

When I work with clients who are looking to increase their self-expression, it is fairly common for them to talk about wanting to write a book. We all have life journeys and lessons that we can learn from each other, so this makes perfect sense. Using emerald green is an excellent tool for speeding up the writing process. Having said that, keep in mind writing is only one form of expressing our unique journey on the planet.

In my opinion, the urge to write a book is more about wanting to feel validated for our experiences than about releasing our inner author. Unless you are already writing regularly, there is a chance that you may seek the validation rather than the creative outlet. When writing is your preferred form of creative expression, it will manifest in many other forms before a book happens. Your words will pour from you naturally, in journals, poems, blogs, stories, and articles. I am not saying this to discourage you from publishing a book. By all means, go for it if you feel motivated! I am just saying that there are many ways to validate your experiences artistically.

Writing a book is not the end goal for creative expression of the written word, it is just one more way to achieve it.

With emerald green, we invoke the artist within our being, and simultaneously heighten our communication skills. It is easy for us to observe a piece of art by another person and think of all the ways we would do it differently. But to be an artist who is putting themselves out there publicly is a whole different story. They must develop an extremely thick skin or risk being discouraged by naysayers.

In our case, we don't have to worry about this. I am not saying that in order to use emerald green successfully, you should go out and express yourself in a major public forum. My goal for this activation is to help you realize your creativity can be as private or public as you want it to be. It does not matter who sees the product of your artistic endeavors as long as you are expressing yourself.

Sharing and communicating your vision to people on the planet brings up many feelings for people, which I totally understand. No one wants to feel judged by others, and there is also the desire to just blend in. If you feel strongly about this, you may want to alternate between working with blue and emerald. With blue, you have made a clear connection to your fear and desire for truth. Now as you access green, you give yourself freedom to fully express all aspects of yourself.

When you activate emerald green, you may notice the color takes on different hues each time. The shades that you see may evolve as you continue to work with each following energy. This is very normal and actually a good sign. It means your process with color is evolving. There is so much depth and wisdom with every color. Let each hue and shade take you to a different place.

SPIRITUAL ACTIVATION NOTES

When I spiritually activated emerald green, it helped me discover my personal favorite form of creative expression. I was born into a very artistic family. My sister, father, and mother all painted quite well, without any kind of formal training. I took an art class with my sister and dad when I was a teenager, naturally assuming that I would be similarly artistic. We each sat down in front of a small blank canvas and were told to paint a still life. There was a tray of fruit artfully arranged in the middle of the room, and we were supposed to paint our own interpretation of it.

After working on my still life for a while, I took a step back to get some perspective. I have a clear memory of looking over at my family's canvases and seeing that their apples and oranges had beautiful softly defined shadows and highlights. My canvas, on the other hand, looked more like I had been painting with my feet instead of my hands.

I immediately felt self-critical about not being as naturally comfortable with a paintbrush as the rest of my family. But more importantly, I was surprised and disappointed that painting as a medium did not satisfy my creative urge. I was certain genetics would have made me a great painter. If painting brought my family so much joy, then surely I should feel the same way—right?

Understanding that we are all individuals who are creatively inspired by different things turned out to be a great lesson for me. I loved spending quiet time with my family but did not feel drawn to doing so with them in the context of painting. Once I realized painting wasn't my chosen area of expression, I had to trust that at some point my creative passion would reveal itself. It was only later, when I began activating emerald green, that I discovered my truest expression of creativity.

Looking back, I see that I had always loved telling stories through the written word. I kept a journal and enjoyed noting my life experiences in it. I loved reading and appreciated reading other people's words as well. Once I remembered the joy of writing, I knew I needed to commit myself to doing it regularly. From blogs to letters, e-mail, and books, I jumped right in to all kinds of writing. My creativity did not involve painting in the end, but it certainly involved color! Instead of painting on a canvas, I paint my own energy with a rainbow of color.

SPIRITUAL ACTIVATION EXERCISE: AWAKEN YOUR INNER ARTIST

This exercise takes us back to memories of childhood, because our early years are when most of us had more time and freedom to use our imagination. Remember, every child is an artist. Using your life experiences as a map, think back to a time when creativity was a normal part of your day.

After spiritually activating green, take a few moments to remember your earliest memories of being creative. Your goal is to invoke a creative hobby that you enjoyed before life exposed you to the all-too-common feelings of self-consciousness or vulnerability. Maybe you were in a play and you really enjoyed portraying a character onstage. Maybe you have a fond memory of carving something in woodworking class or drawing in your notebook after school. You came home beaming with pride to share something you created with your family. Perhaps it was as simple as playing with the dolls in your room and creating a fantasy world. This step is simply about identifying where your creativity has expressed itself before so that you can draw from that energy again. You will know you have found the right creative outlet because it will bring a smile to your face and make you feel good, causing green energy to flow through you.

Re-create the source of your past creative joy at least once a week as you activate emerald. But by all means, do it as often as you like if you feel inspired. Examples of these activities could include:

- Drawing
- Singing
- Pottery or sculpting

To help reactivate your personal expression of joy, ask yourself where you could insert traces of that energy into your current life. This may be a challenge, depending on your circumstances, but remember, there is no wrong way to do this exercise. We are helping to awaken any deep-rooted creativity that may have gone dormant within you.

For me, I was a storyteller as a child. I loved relaying a story to my friends before class and feeling the exchange of energy through expressing myself. Some of my happiest childhood memories involve telling ghost stories around a bonfire at summer camp. I loved knowing I could invoke feelings and sensations with my words. I also loved listening to others make up stories that could take us on a journey together. I often use those kinds of memories to trigger creative energy in my current life. If I were to re-create this energy today, I might write out a fictional story based on anything that inspired me in the moment. I would do it on loose-leaf paper, not in my journal, to remind myself that my goal is to activate creative green energy and not to "create" something lasting. This removes all pressure and allows the exercise to flow freely.

UNIVERSAL ACTIVATION NOTES (AKA "I SPY" WITH MY INTUITIVE EYE)

Emerald green is a powerful color for universal activation, because it works very quickly and can easily be seen in any natural setting where plants are visible. When you start to see deep, rich green energy in your life, let this be a reminder to fully express yourself. Every time this color enters your visual landscape, it is an opportunity to connect with the creative side of your being. If you are enjoying a meal and see a green vegetable, pause for a moment to appreciate your unique expression of creativity. If you are in a meeting with someone who is wearing green, allow that to enhance your communication skills with them. When you notice emerald green, your soul is telling you it would like a dose of this energy. Once you begin to make the connection between colors and their energy, this will become a powerful tool in helping you to gauge which energies you need in any given moment. Emerald green will help you see the beauty in life and appreciate creative expression of all kinds.

A simple way to universally activate emerald green is to change the background of your computer or phone to a rich emerald green for a boost of creative energy. I particularly love doing this when I am writing, as I will constantly see the color green as I am typing away. The green background can be an image of nature, or it can be just a solid green if you like. Various studies have shown that seeing green heightens creativity and communication. Your only limit is your creativity, which is now growing and expanding!

UNIVERSAL ACTIVATION EXERCISE: AN ARTIST'S DATE

This exercise is an easy and fun way to engage a new artistic process. An artist's date is any kind of creative activity that you have never tried before. Our goal here is to open new outlets of personal expression for you. Although there is no guarantee you will love the activity, an artist's date may release new bursts of creativity in other areas of your life. There is also the chance you will discover an enjoyable way to express your creativity that you never thought of before.

Set an intention that you will commit to an artist's date in the next seven days, utilizing the power of universal activation. Keep your eyes open to signs from green energy, and listen when it speaks to you as you look for your artist's date. Perhaps you walk into a painting studio to inquire about their afternoon workshops, and the teacher is wearing a green necklace. Or maybe you are interested in taking a weekend dance class, and you happen to drive by a place near your home called Green Dance Studio. Be open to receiving these messages through color, and you will learn how to spot them more quickly.

The only requirement is that you choose an artist's date that is unusual for you. You are trying to stimulate a different part of your creative consciousness than you normally would. There are no rules to this endeavor. From scrapbooking to making jewelry, taking a cooking class to anything else, how you engage your creative side is completely up to you.

Potential options include:

- Participating in a half-day writing retreat
- Taking a calligraphy workshop
- Trying out an improvised comedy intensive

EMERALD GREEN AFFIRMATION

MY UNIQUE CREATIVITY FLOWS THROUGH ME FREELY.

PHYSICAL ACTIVATION NOTES

As emerald green is also close to the color of mature plants and healthy grass, it is very easy to utilize nature in your color props. I have a variety of potted plants in my house, and I often sit near them or touch them when I write. Plants are a terrific way to bring the color green into your home and workspace.

Another fun way to incorporate the energy of emerald green into your day is to eat it! One of my clients told me she often uses food as a way to boost her work with specific colors, and I think this is a fantastic idea. We not only look at the foods we eat before ingesting them, but we literally absorb their colors into our physical body. And thanks to the variety of green vegetables in the world, your diet can be a truly physical manifestation of taking in emerald energy.

Some emerald green color props you could incorporate into your day include:

- **Plants.** What better way to invoke green energy than by keeping a fresh plant in your home?

- **Your computer background.** If you do any kind of writing, set your computer background to something green, and touch it for a boost of creative energy.

- **A green notebook.** Since green is all about creative expression, try using a green notebook to hold your ideas and creative thoughts.

PHYSICAL ACTIVATION EXERCISE: EAT YOUR GREENS

The purpose of this exercise is to give you a fun way to express your creativity. We all have to eat, so why not activate emerald green at the same time?

Think of a meal you can prepare that showcases the color green. It could be anything from a salad to a spinach wrap, or just about anything else. Some of my favorite emerald green veggies include:

- Spinach
- Broccoli
- Brussels sprouts

As you prepare the meal, make sure to touch each vegetable with the intention of activating your creative spirit.

You can actually use this exercise idea with every color. I also love to intentionally mix foods with different colors, depending on which energy I am activating.

THE SHADOW SIDE OF EMERALD GREEN

The shadow side of emerald green is blocked creativity and communication. If you find yourself saying "I am not a creative person" or "I have nothing to share with the world," then you may be dealing with the shadow side of this color. Although it may seem like it only affects creativity, ignoring emerald green can negatively impact relationships or any elements of your life where your expression may be stunted.

I mentioned your creativity can be expressed as publicly or privately as you like. The shadow side of emerald green fools us into thinking our unique voice is not worthy

of being heard. For example, one of my clients, Jen, identi-
fied as a secret poet. She loved writing poetry as a teenager
and found it to be a cathartic form of journaling her experiences. However, as an adult in Middle America making her
living as a bookkeeper, this was a side of herself she came to
think of as childish. Even her closest friends weren't aware of
her past outlet for self-expression. She had been outgoing in
high school, but as an adult she had become more quiet and
reserved. Something as simple as poetry was hidden away
like it was an addiction or a skeleton in her closet.

She came to me for coaching because she had a strained
relationship with her husband, Brian, and wanted help. Jen
found it easier to bottle up her feelings than to express them,
which ultimately left Brian feeling like he didn't understand
her. Although he meant well, Brian assumed Jen would tell
him if something was bothering her, the way she used to
when they were first dating.

Rather than focusing directly on Jen's relationship, I felt
she would benefit from first sharing her creative side with
others. Tuning in to her energy, I could see dark green hov-
ering above her physical body. That her aura was so disconnected from her body told me she had a strained relationship
with green energy and self-expression. It seemed to me that
with such strong artistic energy clearly radiating from her,
stuffing it away was shutting down her ability to communicate from her core.

I had her try out the "Awaken Your Inner Artist" exercise,
which revealed strong, happy memories of writing poetry. Jen
even pulled out some of her old poetry journals that she had
saved in a box of mementos. Seeing sparks of joy as she held
those journals, I thought Jen should try to awaken her inner
poet again to see how it feels. I had a hunch communicating

through poetry to others could be just as cathartic as when she first wrote her poems alone in her room.

When it was time for her to express herself, Jen committed to writing poetry again. She found a local writers' workshop where she could practice once a week, and she fell head over heels in love with the process. Jen continued activating emerald green and later reported the experience not only satisfied her creatively but also brought her closer to her husband. She had shown him the poems that she worked on, some of which were about their relationship. In them, she spoke of her love for him and her fear of being rejected for being herself. Seeing Jen express her vulnerability through poetry helped Brian become more communicative with his own feelings. He even attended an open mike night where she read her poems, and he was excited to be able to support his wife. Communicating who you are as a unique individual will translate positively throughout all areas of your life.

CHAPTER 7

❖

PURPLE

QUALITIES: Leadership, destiny, and purpose
SHADOW SIDE: Lack of direction; indecisiveness

Regal purple has had a long, worldwide association with leadership energy. In fact, it leads as one of the very first colors ever used in ancient art, dating back to 25,000 B.C.E. in French Neolithic sites. Purple became the color of choice for various leaders such as royalty, priests, nobles, and officers throughout the world, starting in the 15th century in the Mediterranean. Purple is the color used by the British royal family, and other royalty in Europe for special occasions. Purple robes are often worn at graduation ceremonies by theology students who intend to lead in spiritual thought. Purple is the color I turn to whenever I want to feel especially self-assured and confident in my decisions.

In Japan, purple is the color of the aristocratic family and the emperor. In China, purple is associated with spiritual awareness and strength, the classic traits of a leader. In Chinese painting, purple is the symbolic color of achieving harmony in the universe, as it is a combination of blue and red (yin and yang).

Purple was even mentioned in the Old Testament. In the book of Exodus, Moses is told by God to have the Israelites bring him offerings that include purple cloth, to be used in the Tabernacle and in the making of religious clothing of priests. (I mean, if it's good enough for God . . .) And Jesus, on the day of his crucifixion, was dressed in purple by the Roman troops. Although their intention was to mock his claim that he was "King of the Jews," the Romans subconsciously acknowledged Jesus's leadership by dressing him in the color of leadership and destiny.

Alexander the Great, one of the greatest military leaders in recorded history, wore purple to important ceremonies. And King Solomon was said to have decorated the Temple of Jerusalem in rich purple cloth. During the Roman Republic, any general who led his forces in a successful battle wore a purple toga as a public sign of honor. And in the United States, a purple heart is usually seen as a sign of bravery, being awarded to those in the military who are wounded in combat.

In the early 1900s, purple became associated with people who led all kinds of social progress. It was one of the main colors of the women's suffrage movement, the courageous fight for women's right to vote. To honor the suffragettes, purple was the representative color of the women's liberation movement in the 1970s, which made major progress toward establishing equality for all women.

Purple is a useful color if you are grappling with finding your purpose. "What is my purpose?" is a question I hear from clients several times a day. If finding your purpose is something you are grappling with, purple is a useful color to help you determine what it is. I find a lack of purpose tends to also include a general sense of feeling lost, so building up some leadership energy will help you to break this pattern. After all, leadership qualities are required for us to separate from the pack and stand on our own. In all my years as a psychic and life coach, the concept of our destiny is one of my clients' most common existential questions. Even I have asked myself from time to time, *Why am I here? What is the point of all this? What am I supposed to be doing with my life?*

As a young adult, I was certain my ultimate purpose was to be a psychic and spiritual teacher. But now that I am further along on my spiritual journey, that idea seems somewhat ego-driven. In my early twenties, I must admit I liked the attention I received for being a psychic. It didn't matter if I was talking to a believer or a nonbeliever. Whenever I was asked what I did for my job, the answer always made heads turn.

"But how do you earn a living?" someone might ask, as a follow-up.

"Um, as a psychic." It seemed to baffle people, as if I had told them that I sell beepers for a living.

Even though being a psychic is very much a part of my purpose, it was also a form of rebellion. When I scan my choices and life back then, I now realize I was in a lot of pain. I was still in the closet, very overweight, and not really in alignment with my destiny or purpose at all. The implications of the grand statement "I am a psychic" seemed to make people (including myself) think I was quite connected to my purpose. This is when I realized that our job is not the same thing as our destiny.

When I use purple to meditate on my purpose these days, the answer that feels right is, I am here to empower other people to live a better life. I feel happiest when I can validate the experiences of others and offer guidance in any way that is helpful. I am lucky my work allows me to do this regularly, but I would still be as driven by the same purpose if I were an attorney, an accountant, or had any other job. Just to be clear, I absolutely love my work and get much fulfillment from helping people. But my career does not define the entirety of my being. Rather, it is a tool to help me express my purpose.

Depending on your life circumstances, your job may be nothing more than a way to help you pay the bills and support your family. There is absolutely nothing wrong with this, and it would be unrealistic to assume otherwise. I have various clients who run successful companies, but their actual life purpose exists outside of work. And yet client after client will ask me what their purpose is in direct relation to their job.

What if there is a deeper reason for being on the planet? Perhaps the concept of our purpose is more profound than anyone can imagine. According to Buddhist thought, *dukkha*, or suffering, is caused by our desire to hold on to things that are constantly changing. We must be aware our purpose will continue to change throughout our lives, just like our job may change.

I recently had a reading with a man in his midfifties named Bill.

"Well, mornin'," Bill said with the deepest southern drawl I have ever heard. Which says a lot, given that I lived in Texas for five years.

"Hi, Bill, nice to meet you! Have you ever had an intuitive reading before?" I asked.

"No sir."

"How did you hear about me?"

"I can't remember how I heard 'bout y'all."

I took him through a brief meditation that I do at the beginning of every session. This process helps to clear my energy and prepares me to receive any information that may come through about my client. Then I began the reading.

"Bill, please say your name three times for me."

"Bill, Bill, Bill."

The moment Bill uttered the first sound of his name, my mind's eye was flooded with deep, rich purple energy. I sat up straight in my chair and wrote down on my pad in front of me: *I am in the presence of greatness.*

"Bill, as soon as you say your name, I see the most brilliant purple energy around you. I define purple as the color of leadership and destiny. Purple helps us to align with our purpose. It's hard for me to explain, but when I tune in to your energy, I feel taller, stronger, and somehow more confident."

"That's funny, because I am not feeling like much of a leader right now."

Bill's response surprised me. His energy came across as secure and fully engaged. Usually, if someone is insecure or lacks confidence, I have the opposite feeling of what I was experiencing with Bill. I might slouch in my chair or feel a nervous rush or a sense of confusion. It's possible that he might not see himself the way the world perceives him. And there's always a chance I am not connecting with his energy. That's the thing about intuition. It is a healing *art*, not an exact science. If a client's response doesn't fit my psychic impression, I go back and double-check my intuition. In the event what I am saying does not resonate for the client, I will usually end the reading and refund their payment.

"The sense that I get, Bill, is that you are quite successful financially. I am drawn to talk about the work aspect of your life, which is dominant in your energy. You have developed quite a family at work, and it seems like you are great at highlighting the strengths of a whole team of people. When I focus on your career, my heart feels full and satisfied, which would mean your relationships there are balanced. You are great at not only leading people but also bringing them together. It feels like your work identity has allowed you to be fully engaged in your life purpose. Does this make sense?"

"It's funny you say 'family,' because I use that word all the time. I owned a construction company in Houston, and I always talked about my team as *family*. We held weekly meetings with the 'work family.' I never liked calling them my employees because I felt like we were building something together as equals. Hell, there were some days that I was with them more than with my own flesh and blood."

This is a moment I call psychic Tourette's syndrome. It's not like Bill's spirit guides whispered in my ear, *He refers to the people that he works with as his family*. But rather, a key word will float through my being, and I am usually not even aware of how much it means to the individual I am speaking to until I say it out loud. Purple also helps me in these moments because it requires a leap of faith to talk about an intuitive message that is coming through. It doesn't matter if I am wrong; what matters most is that I deliver the message.

"So why aren't you feeling confident? I would imagine that owning a successful business and being the team leader would be extremely validating."

"That's exactly why I wanted to speak with you. I recently sold my company, and without it—well, I am feeling a little lost. Building a business I could sell was always the end game for me. But now that I've done it, I don't feel the way I thought I would."

We spent a few minutes talking about why he decided to sell his construction company. Bill's father abandoned the family when Bill was just a baby. The responsibility of raising Bill and his older sister was left completely up to his mother. She did her best to provide for the family, but was without any financial support or consistent job. They were constantly on the verge of homelessness. In light of such a stressful upbringing, Bill vowed never to repeat this experience and grew up determined to lead his family to prosperity. As he spoke, swirls of purple energy pulsed around his head and shoulders. I could see his leadership energy had been awakened early and ran deep.

Bill explained that as soon as he graduated high school, he got hired doing physical labor at a local construction company. Each day, he focused on his main goal of being the best employee on the construction site, learning as much as he could about his job. He soon impressed the owner, who promoted him. His supportive boss regularly told him what a good job he was doing, which profoundly boosted Bill's confidence. Seeing real promise, Bill's boss lent him the money to go to school so he could get a general contractor's license. He remained laser-focused for years and led his family to prosperity, a classic purple characteristic. One day, after building up enough credit to qualify for a bank loan, Bill started his own successful construction company, where he made sure to be just as supportive of his own employees as his boss was of him. Through sheer will and his own leadership abilities, Bill was able to become a completely self-made man. He built his mother a beautiful house on a lake and took care of her the way he had always wanted to.

But as soon as he came to the end of his story, the purple energy that had surrounded Bill's head drifted up and away from him. It hovered above his body, disconnected from him. When this happens during a reading, I know the client is currently struggling with this particular energy.

Bill had created a business from scratch and led a whole team of people to success. But, as he put it, he wasn't quite sure about his identity anymore. The novelty of playing golf every day was wearing off, and he was craving a purpose.

"You know, before, everyone knew me for my job. My clients were my friends. My team was really part of my family. And now what?"

"Bill, do me a favor. Close your eyes and take a deep breath. I want you to picture your entire body surrounded by purple light. As you breathe, feel that purple light fill the room you are in right now. Now I am going to ask you a question, and I want to say the first thing that pops into your mind. What about your job made you the most happy?"

"Training people."

"What do you mean by 'training people'?"

Bill opened his eyes and looked at me. "I started my life on the bottom. I got to where I am through hard work and have done pretty well for myself. I was lucky to benefit from the kindness of people who were willing to train me along the way. I was hungry to succeed, and my first boss was nice enough to support me. I never forgot that, and I made sure to pass it on at my company. I think that's what I miss the most."

In this moment, Bill's soul was sending clear messages about his purpose. He wanted to teach people how to help themselves, which I completely understand, because that is similar to my own purpose. He had been used to teaching and helping others succeed at work, but he felt like this purpose was taken away after selling the company. Bill needed to learn he could still express his purpose in various life situations, and purple energy was the perfect way to facilitate that awakening. Purpose does not have to come only through career. I asked Bill what was taking up most of his time since retiring.

"I have been spending more time at the gym. I like to keep busy, and it helps me get rid of my extra energy. I also started reading about nutrition and how to eat better. Some of my friends have started to ask for help with getting healthy."

Bill was intuitively clear about his purpose, and since he sold his company, he had already begun manifesting new ways of living that purpose. But his attachment to his work identity was keeping him from seeing that his purpose could live on separately from work. Based on what he had told me at the start of our session, the issue was helping him integrate feeling confident about it.

Bill ended up doing a few coaching sessions with me, and we really explored his attachment to what it meant to be successful. I had him try the "What Is My Purpose?" exercise below, to help him connect with his true calling. The deeper we went, the more he realized it was more than work that made him feel good. The real joy came from empowering others to empower themselves. When Bill was expressing this, he felt fully connected to his passion.

With this information clear, we outlined a plan to help Bill honor his purpose. He contacted a few of his friends who wanted help with getting in shape and made a plan to meet with them regularly at the gym so he could train them. He did this for free because he just wanted to be helpful to his friends. Bill then made detailed meal plans for them to follow so they knew when and how to best nourish their bodies. He also established a scholarship fund at the school where he got his contractor's license, which would empower others by giving them the same financial opportunities that he was given. By the end of our time together, Bill's purple energy was radiating as powerfully as ever.

Working with purple energy helps us to find our soul's destiny and discover what makes us feel connected to our true self. There is an illusion that our destiny is connected to our career. For some, this can be true. If we listen to a musician or poet perform, we can feel their joy and know that they have merged their passion with their work. But our destiny and our purpose is multifaceted. I used to think my destiny was to be a psychic and a spiritual teacher, and I think that this is an integral part of my journey. But my intuition and desire to help people could have manifested no matter what I did for a living. And I would soon find that out firsthand.

In the winter of 2013, I found myself co-hosting a live late-night talk show on TV. I am naturally chatty and don't take myself too seriously, which I think helps the topic of intuition be more relatable. I have always enjoyed blending the worlds of spirituality and pop culture. After a day of working with clients and processing energy, one of the ways I love to relax is to watch a cooking show, something about home decorating, or any other lighthearted entertainment. I know many of my clients assume I spend my nights meditating in the lotus position. But after spending my entire day working in the spiritual world, I need a break from it to create a sense of balance.

A producer had seen one of my videos on YouTube and called me for a meeting. The world of television has presented itself to me throughout my life, and I am always open to opportunities that can help expose a wider audience of people to the power of color. The producer was working on building a team of experts that would give live advice to callers about sex and relationships. The panel was to include radio personality Heidi Hamilton, Dr. Mike Dow, adult-film star Katie Morgan, and me.

Yes, you read that correctly. This was definitely *not* my usual circle of spiritual colleagues, and I was admittedly concerned about working with an adult-video actress. The idea was to offer a wide range of dating advice that would help people find lasting love. I came home and told David about the opportunity, along with my hesitations. I had been spiritually activating purple and was clear in my intended purpose of helping others by sharing my work in a lighthearted way. Ultimately, after activating purple I decided this would be a great opportunity to connect with an entirely new audience and still stay true to my purpose. Besides, who am I to judge someone else's job? The ironic part is that after we met, Katie told me she was just as hesitant about working with a psychic. Go figure.

I ended up being hired to co-host *That Sex Show*, which lasted for about 60 episodes on the Logo channel. I often activated purple before going onstage every night. In the fast-paced atmosphere of live television, I needed to be extremely focused on my purpose. There is one particular night I specifically recall because it was related to finding my purpose. At the end of one of our shows, I remember exiting the stage and heading down a corridor to the makeup room to change into my regular clothes. As I rounded a corner, one of the studio's security guards was staring right at me. He was a sweet guy and looked to be about in his late fifties. He was wearing a dark suit and an earpiece, which always makes everything seem fancy. He was smiling, so I smiled back.

"You know you are destined to do this right?"

I stopped dead in my tracks. "What?"

"You were born to do this."

He went on to explain that I said something to one of our callers that had stuck with him. A young man had called in because he was concerned about his girlfriend. They were fighting a lot, and he thought she was going to leave him. Anytime she tried to talk about the issues at her stressful job, he would immediately fire off a series of potential solutions. She kept telling him that he wasn't there for her emotionally, while he was getting frustrated and confused by her reactions.

I had advised the caller that his job in those moments was not to try to fix his girlfriend's problems. She was a strong adult and could certainly handle her colleagues at work. What she needed was for him to bear witness to her feelings.

So many men make the well-intentioned mistake of trying to swoop in and fix everything, which is often misconstrued by their partners as "not listening." I explained that all she wanted was for him to validate her feelings, which meant saying something like "Wow, that sounds really tough" if she was venting about her job. Being heard is what so many of us crave. After finishing this story, the security guard told me that he tried this with his own wife and it worked incredibly well. Chills went down my back because I was living my purpose and actually had the privilege of helping someone. I smiled and thanked him.

When I replay that story in my mind, it brings me such a sense of joy. As I have worked with purple energy in my life, it has taught me such a deep understanding about purpose and destiny. I want to help support and empower people toward living a better life. Co-hosting a TV show was not my life purpose, but it did serve as a vehicle to help me express that purpose. What I know about that experience is I was given the chance to help people, whether it was a viewer or the security guard backstage. I was an openly gay intuitive life coach on national TV, providing guidance in the best way I know how. And the beauty of purpose is that even though the show was canceled, I still get to do this every day in my work, as well as in my personal life.

Our destiny and purpose cannot be defined by one specific job. It is an energy that morphs and transforms depending on our life circumstances. Our job is to honor that energy, and purple helps us find the pathway to doing that.

ACTIVATING PURPLE NOTES

WHAT IS MY PURPOSE?

When you activate purple, people will see a side of you that is most connected to your destiny. This leadership energy exists in all of us, but we may not know how to draw the connection between leadership and our purpose if we are not looking for it. Purple turns the volume up on this energy and helps us find out why we are here. I often comment if I notice that someone seems to be in their power, or "in the zone." It is inspiring to see someone giving their best in any area, living in their light, and being fully connected to their journey.

If you are comfortable with attention, then purple will be easy and familiar. But if receiving attention is something that is new for you, then activating this energy may feel a bit odd at first (see the shadow side below). Nonetheless, purple is even more important for you to activate in this case. You can always control how much leadership you want to take on. The most important part of activating purple is to give yourself permission to be more visible so you can connect with your destiny.

It is human nature to look up to accomplished people, and this is easiest to see in the business world. Although a fancy diploma may help with certain business skills, leadership energy is what we all respect and react to the most. Many people who are successful in business do not have a formal education, but what they lack in a title is more than made up for by their confidence. They know what they want to achieve, and this energy swirls around them, moving unseen forces into place to help make it so. Purple energy can be applied throughout all areas of your life and will help the people around you to relax, because they will feel more confident in your decisions.

When activating purple, you will notice yourself standing a little bit taller, stronger, and having a deeper sense of self as you work with this regal color. Purple is what I would describe as a more sophisticated energy, and it is also a very social color.

SPIRITUAL ACTIVATION NOTES

We are all a combination of various energies, and sometimes they conflict. There is a part of each of us that is connected to divine, pure, purple wisdom. I believe when we connect with this energy, we all know the true best choice for stepping into our destiny. This is the place where our true leadership and purpose comes from. When clients awaken their sense of purpose during a session, they are usually able to answer their own pressing life questions with perfect clarity. This is precisely why I titled my first book *But You Knew That Already*. I believe that we already possess the answers we need to find our ultimate path, if only we can awaken that inner wisdom.

But there is a reason why this is easier said than done. We are all human, just trying to keep our heads down and get through life in the easiest way possible. Depending on where you are on your path, you may need a boost so you can find your path more easily.

When it comes to receiving the message of your ultimate purpose, keep yourself open to wisdom from a variety of sources, and take the best from each one. My wise friend Colette Baron-Reid, known as the Oracle, has personally helped me find clarity on my purpose. And Danielle LaPorte offers fantastic online programs that can help you along as you seek out your destiny. There are many other useful resources online that can help you on your journey.

Spiritually activate purple through meditation as you continue along on your path toward purpose. Doing so will help your inner leader speak up so you hear it clearly when you have found what your soul is looking for. Ultimately, your inner leader will take you to the answer.

The most common response my clients report from activating purple is that people may ask you for your opinion more often. This can manifest in a variety of ways, from strangers asking for directions to friends seeking guidance in their life. This is because purple helps the leader in you to rise to the surface.

SPIRITUAL ACTIVATION EXERCISE: WHAT IS MY PURPOSE?

Finding our purpose on the planet means asking one of the most existential questions that can be asked. The search for meaning helps us understand why we are here on the planet and what we are supposed to do. It is a wonderful blessing if our job allows us to fulfill our purpose, but there are other ways to express our destiny aside from work.

Go through the process of spiritually activating purple in meditation. Once you have grounded purple energy throughout your body, ask your higher self to present what you do for others that brings *you* the most joy. This can be based on a memory or it can simply come as a message that you need to receive. Examples could include:

- Making people laugh
- Helping others overcome grief
- Nourishing bodies through the creation of healthy food

Do not rush yourself if the answer does not come right away. You can ask this question as often as you spiritually activate purple. The main goal is to focus on what makes you feel good.

UNIVERSAL ACTIVATION NOTES (AKA "I SPY" WITH MY INTUITIVE EYE)

Whenever you see purple, try to improve your posture and stand with confidence. A leader who is connected to their purpose stands with grace, pride, and elegance. When you see this color, whether on purpose or by accident, take a deep breath and stand taller with your shoulders back. You can visualize yourself as a military general, a judge in a courtroom, or any kind of leader who would stand tall with pride.

Notice your reaction to this. How does it feel to stand tall? How does it feel to be proud? How does it feel to gracefully accept the attention *you deserve*? You will notice slight physical reactions to these questions. Your body may contract or relax. You may tense up and resist the idea, depending on your self-esteem. Any or all of these reactions are great opportunities to fully integrate into your destiny.

UNIVERSAL ACTIVATION EXERCISE: WHAT WOULD A LEADER DO?

This exercise will help you regularly boost your leadership qualities throughout the day. The reason is that it refocuses your life through a lens of decisive purpose, and that can be challenging if you are not used to harnessing purple leadership energy. I have found it is much easier to give good counsel and advice to friends on their lives. Yet it can be more complicated to make these same good choices when it comes to your own best interests. This exercise will sharpen decisive traits that will help you claim your true purpose.

The purpose of this is to connect with your inner leader and provide your own source of guidance. As you invoke your leader with purple energy, the part of you that is connected to its destiny will rise to the surface and help you find the answer. Since the universal activation process involves setting an intention to notice purple, this exercise will be ongoing as you work with it throughout your day.

Ask yourself to think of an area where you feel indecisive or stuck. First, write the question out. You can write it on a piece of paper or in your phone. I find writing things down on paper helps ground them in my consciousness, but any format will work. This question can be any area where you would like a boost of leadership energy. Here are some examples:

- Why do I feel like I am at a dead end in my job?

- Why am I lonely so often?

Set an intention to think of your question whenever you notice purple during your day. Allow the universe to present how your inner leader would handle the situation at hand. If you have any trouble receiving an answer, continue to reactivate purple anytime you see it, keeping your question in mind. Examples of answers that might come up would be:

- You subconsciously don't believe your voice matters, so you choose not to speak up or offer your thoughts for fear of being rejected. This causes a cycle where you never step out of your comfort zone, even if you have ideas that could be helpful to others.

133

- You are shy, so you stick with the group of people you already know from childhood, even though you have grown apart and do not enjoy how much they gossip. Try joining a Meetup group that focuses on a hobby you like.

Keep these answers in mind as you continue activating purple. The intention here is to continually strengthen that inner leader so you can begin making decisions from that place of power. Each time you strengthen your own leadership energy, it will inspire you to take the steps your inner leader wants.

PURPLE AFFIRMATION

I AM CONNECTED TO MY DESTINY.

PHYSICAL ACTIVATION NOTES

I find physical activations to be particularly useful with purple because we can touch our color props at the precise moment when we need a boost of purple decisiveness, leadership, and destiny. With this in mind, color props such as jewelry or healing stones are useful with purple. Amethyst is a popular purple crystal in the New Age community, and I love it for physically activating purple energy. I have a large amethyst crystal in my office that I like to touch throughout my work day. If I am distracted or frustrated for any reason, I find that touching the purple amethyst helps clarify my purpose before I work with clients. I like knowing that medieval European soldiers often wore amethyst to keep a powerful sense of calm during war. I feel purple energy helped them remain steadfast during such turbulent times. Although I love purple amethyst, touching any kind of purple color prop will also activate this energy within you.

I recently co-hosted a retreat in Hawaii with my dear friend Alan Cohen. Alan is a prolific author of dozens of wonderful New Age books. He has a natural grace about him and is also the epitome of purple energy. Alan exudes a natural, relaxed confidence when he teaches. He is a spiritual teacher that inspires others to connect with their own guidance. Our retreat, "The Guru in You," was created with the intention of carving out a sacred space for all of our students to find their true purpose. We wanted them to realize that God, wisdom, and the true guru already lived in their hearts.

On the last day—or graduation day, as Alan liked to call it—we wanted to send each participant home with a reminder of their newly empowered inner guru. The scent of Hawaiian frangipani wafted through the air as we handed out bracelets with colorful beads. The top seven beads represented each chakra, and the remaining beads were all purple. The goal was to give each participant a lasting visual representation of their own innate leadership and guidance. I loved this idea and regularly wear my bracelet to physically activate purple. I caress the purple beads anytime I want to be reminded of my inner leader.

Some purple color props you could incorporate into your day include:

- **Purple flowers.** I love using flowers as color props for all colors, but they are particularly beautiful for purple. Snapdragon, verbena, and pansies are only a few of the glorious manifestations of purple in the flower kingdom.

- **Amethyst.** Although crystals come in every color, amethyst is the one I love having in my office the most.

- **Purple accessories.** Purple is a great color to wear in work situations. If you are applying for a new job, have a presentation, or for any reason need to command authority and power, use purple accessories as a color prop to invoke that energy.

PHYSICAL ACTIVATION EXERCISE: YOUR TWIN LEADER

This exercise may require a bit more effort because it specifically requires action steps, but it is well worth your time. I find it is often easier to connect with our power if we begin by pretending we are advising another person. This helps to sidestep any limiting thoughts or beliefs until after we access our wisdom.

1. Select a color prop to use for this exercise and hold it in your hands. After you feel connected to purple, I want you to close your eyes and imagine you have an exact duplicate of yourself somewhere in the world. They are living the exact same life as you, with the exact same experiences. Using this other version of yourself, I want you to zoom in and take a bird's-eye view of this person's life. How often do they step into a leadership role? Are they expressing their opinions truthfully? Write down the areas

or specific instances where they could showcase more leadership qualities. Examples might be:

- Decide to live healthier and begin an exercise program, even if their family is not interested in joining them.

- Take steps toward starting the online business they have been dreaming about.

2. When I think of examples of a leader, I picture someone who might run a company or motivate others. Or in every family, there is always a member who tends to plan the social schedules, trips, and reunions. With these examples in mind, focus on your twin and determine if they are allowing their leader to come through.

3. List at least one action your twin could take to step into their power. Examples include:

- If they are shy and have a friend's birthday party coming up, they could offer to host, organize, or oversee it.

- Plan an outing with a group of friends.

- Initiate a social gathering at work.

4. Challenge *yourself* to take this leadership step.

The idea is to recognize any leadership opportunity, big or small, and allow yourself to say yes. This is how you strengthen purple energy in your life. I have spent years with clients coming to me and asking me to predict their future. And at the beginning of my career, I believed this was exactly how it worked. If I could just tune in to the map of the universe, I would advise you on how to plot your course. You would have an easy guide to help you stay clear of obstacles while you waited for your destiny to arrive. But this is not the truth of co-creating.

We all help build our reality, and we must take steps to claim our true destiny. Purple helps us realize we can muster up our own leader and make our own destiny. Purple energy helps us set things in motion.

When you are looking for opportunities to take a leadership position, release judgment or expectation of what that means. Oftentimes, the opportunity has been right in front of you, waiting for you to accept the challenge.

THE SHADOW SIDE OF PURPLE

The shadow side of purple is a lack of direction and chronic indecisiveness. Although purple's ultimate message is that of destiny, there are a variety of seemingly minor situations that can stump us if we are struggling with the shadow side of purple energy. The main sign of a purple imbalance is hesitating to make decisions. If you find yourself constantly struggling with choices, big or small, then you know what a purple imbalance feels like. The consequences of purple's shadow side are immediate and pervasive.

An imbalance of purple energy often brings up feelings of regret, which is another classic sign we are uncomfortable accepting our role as leaders in our own lives. When we think of destiny and leadership, we tend to conjure up very grand images and ideas of what this looks like. But on a day-to-day basis, struggling with leadership can boil down to having trouble deciding where to eat lunch. The good news is you can easily work on healing this imbalance by making quicker decisions. Activate purple however you like, and then start with the smallest decisions possible. Whether it's the kind of shampoo you buy or what movie to watch with your spouse, try to use purple to be more decisive. It may not seem relevant, but these choices are related to awakening your inner leader. The more comfortable you become at making these minor decisions, the better you will become at listening to yourself when it comes to bigger life issues.

If you find that activating purple light has made you acknowledge a lack of direction, there is a chance you could take this in a self-critical direction. Self-criticism keeps you stagnant, and it is a trick your mind plays to stop you from making change. Nonetheless, if this happens, you will want to start with smaller, easier leadership qualities to manifest.

I used to love using Franklin planners way back in the day, as they helped me to overcome an imbalance of purple. These day planners were convenient for organizing my life, with to-do lists and reminders. After moving out on my own, I struggled with knowing how to proceed with creating a life for myself. I was on my own earlier than most and was trying to figure out how to be productive. I discovered the joy of lists as motivation to help me achieve my goal of working in the healing arts. For me, my day planner functioned as a leader until I was confident enough to lead myself.

There was a whole system of priorities so I could order my tasks in terms of importance, but I whittled my planner down to a simpler version. I would list literally everything I had done in the morning, and then put a check next to each item:

1. Woke up
2. Made bed
3. Ate breakfast

By the time I got to school, I had a list of at least five accomplishments for the day. When I made my list and took note of what I had done, my energy level would increase. I felt accomplished, and it helped me to keep going. Nowadays, I always use similar lists when I activate purple. Doing so is useful for me in achieving bigger goals in my life. This idea is similar to rewarding a young kid with a sticker for good behavior. The sticker itself doesn't hold any power, yet the child feels a sense of pride when they receive recognition of an accomplishment. If you are struggling with being a leader and feeling connected with your destiny, this could be a helpful tool, along with activating purple. Start by noting your daily routine and accomplishments.

Remember, you are constantly guiding yourself through life. This is no small task. Build from your routine and watch your accomplishments grow.

❖

CHAPTER 8

RUBY RED

QUALITIES: Healthy emotions and relationships
SHADOW SIDE: Emotional imbalance; being oversensitive or disconnected

Red is an inherently emotional color, vibrating from the deepest reaches of our heart. It is the color of blood and therefore also the source of our life force, so red is intrinsically linked with every kind of emotion we may feel. Culturally, this is the color most strongly associated with all emotions, both positive and negative. And while there may be an unlimited range of emotions we can experience as human beings, the unifying theme with red is it makes us feel our emotions more strongly. Working with red will make you more aware of your emotions and how you feel in any given moment.

Throughout history, red has been the color most often associated with strong emotions. It is most commonly thought of in relation to love, sexuality, and emotional joy. Further establishing the emotional element, red roses and red hearts are classic symbols of romantic love. Red is also the color we naturally associate with fire or danger, and this primal, emotional response to red is encoded into all of us. In the English language, there are many common sayings referring to red being an emotional color. For example, "seeing red" indicates anger and "raising the red flag" indicates imminent danger.

In Buddhism, red is one of the colors said to have radiated from the Buddha when he achieved nirvana, or the highest state of enlightenment. Red, in particular, is associated with some of the benefits of practicing Buddhism. These include wisdom, virtue, and dignity. In Asia, red is highly regarded as the color of happiness and joyful prosperity. In the Japanese Shinto religion, the stately gates of shrine (known as torii) are painted a warm red to symbolize the passage from an ordinary place into a spiritual one.

I love examining my own experiences with color alongside scientific studies to see how they compare. When I looked into experiments with red, I found that they demonstrated a consistent heightening of a variety of emotions. A study out of the University of Rochester revealed men were significantly more sexually attracted to women who wore red.[5] This is no surprise if you look at female primates (like chimpanzees), who redden noticeably when they are nearing ovulation. It is nature's way of attracting a mate. But desire is also one of the most powerful emotions that we can feel, so it is fitting it would be stirred up by the color red. Car insurance companies are thought to charge higher premiums for red cars. They assume the driver will be more likely to enjoy thrill seeking through speeding. For the insurers, red signifies you must enjoy heightened emotions like passion and exhilaration.

Brides in India and China wear red wedding dresses as a symbol of purity. In ancient Egypt, red was the color of life itself, and citizens (including Cleopatra) would decorate themselves with red during celebrations. As one of the most common colors for national flags, red is used to symbolize the blood and sacrifice of those who defended their country.

Red is the color that naturally attracts the most attention, so it is the best choice for when we want to connect with others emotionally. It is useful when we want to relate to people and also when we want to reconnect with our own emotional body. If I feel disconnected from a loved one or can sense I am avoiding any uncomfortable feelings in my own life, red is the perfect color for me to work with.

Ruby red is directly connected to our heart center. It represents the root of our emotions and determines how we connect, as well as interact, with others. I often see ruby red around healers and highly empathetic people. When I say *healer*, I am referring to any kind of healing a person can bring about. This often comes from a shaman, surgeon, acupuncturist, massage therapist, or similar type of person. But, ultimately, red has no boundaries when it comes to agents of the healing arts.

As an empath (someone who easily feels the emotions and mental states of others), red is one of the colors I have explored the most. I personally identify as being very sensitive. I have cried tears of joy at weddings of people I barely knew, especially if their loved ones were crying as well. I am also very sensitive to stories in books and to watching the news, movies, and even well-made TV commercials. In therapy, I used to talk about wanting to have thicker skin, but I have come to learn empathy is one of my greatest strengths. Being sensitive means a person has a powerful connection to energy and an evolved emotional intelligence. These are valuable qualities that do not always come naturally to people. If you consider yourself sensitive and can manage it properly, this energy can help you strengthen your relationships to others.

The secret to a healthy relationship with your emotions is learning when and how deeply to access them. As you activate ruby red, you will be exploring your relationship to the profound world of emotions. This color will also help you see the energy exchange you have in the various relationships in your life.

I have always been drawn to people's life stories, and working with red has really helped me to home in on the reasons why. While it may be tedious for some to listen to other people's issues, I love understanding the emotions behind people's decisions and helping them understand their feelings. Before I began coaching and doing intuitive work professionally, I even found myself fascinated by people's stories on TV. Documentaries, memoirs, and first-person narratives of any sort drew me like a magnet.

I used to think this was happening to me without my control, but I now realize that at times I was using it as an escape. This is one of the reasons why some of us can get so invested in the problems of our loved ones. It is also the reason why reality TV is so compelling to many people. Let's be honest: it's way more fun to dissect someone else's life than our own. I can spend hours guiding and teaching others, but my own physical, emotional, and spiritual practice takes a little more effort to get going.

It is important to notice when we are focusing too much on the feelings of other people, because this can be a sign that we may be avoiding our own feelings. This is the beauty of working with ruby energy. It helps us take emotional inventory of our own soul.

Think of your heart center as a bank where you can make deposits and withdrawals. We all have a certain amount of emotional equity in our heart bank, and we must pay attention to what is coming in and going out. When you meet people and form a new relationship, an emotional deposit is created for you both. This deposit varies in size, depending on the energy exchange and connection between you. If you are spending too much time focused on the other people in your life, you may forget to check whether you are giving out more than you are receiving.

In business relationships, it is much easier to monitor an energy exchange. When you are hired for a job, the energy exchange is very clear, because it is usually determined in salary and benefits. You know up front what you are putting in and what you are getting out. But our personal relationships are a little bit harder to monitor. The ultimate goal with red is to have the loved ones in our life engaging in a balanced or equal exchange of energy with us. I'm not saying it needs to be tit for tat, but you should check in with yourself on a regular basis to gauge whether your emotional needs are being cared for and supported. If not, you may end up feeling either somewhat numb or overly emotional to compensate for the lack.

Subconsciously, we create spiritual contracts all the time that lay the foundation for our energetic and emotional exchanges. In my case, I tend to naturally send out a vibe to people that says, "I can listen to you; I can support you; and I will encourage you whenever you need me." This is exactly how I want to come across, but in the past, I would forget to tell people what I needed in return. In my desire to connect, I would just put out unlimited amounts of energy, without ever focusing on myself. Oftentimes, my heart center would then go into spiritual foreclosure or exhaustion because I couldn't meet the requirements.

On the flip side, I was recently working with a coaching client whose name is Rebecca. Rebecca contacted me because she wanted to work on the romantic blocks in her life, but they were indicative of a larger emotional blockage. Rebecca was an entertainment attorney in Los Angeles. She had achieved great success in her career but was struggling to find a romantic partner. I called her phone number at the time of her session, and her assistant placed me on hold as she got Rebecca. From the moment we began our session, I could feel that accessing her emotions was not easy for her.

"How do you let the world and your community know you are looking for a relationship?" I asked Rebecca. This is a common question I first ask clients who are trying to manifest love.

"I'm not sure what you mean about my community. My job keeps me busy most of the time, just like most people's. No one here needs to know about my love life."

"I was referring more to your soul group. Do you have any friends you have told about your desire for a romantic connection?"

"All my old friends have gotten married and have kids. They have better things to do than listen to me complain."

As she spoke, I could see an opaque red energy tightly wound around her head and shoulders. The opaqueness of the aura told me that her relationship with this energy was not flowing freely, and its closeness to her body informed me that she was guarding her emotions.

"If we want to attract a romantic partner and it hasn't happened yet, it's important to get the energy moving by claiming it."

"Well, it is the major theme of my vision board." Rebecca replied.

"Tell me about your vision board."

"I like vision boards. My current vision board is filled with pictures that show the kind of love that I want. I have an image of a happy couple walking on a beach. I also cut out romantic words and pasted them all over the board. The biggest words are *passion, sex, intimacy*, and *support*. Every morning I look at the board and imagine being in love. It's funny, too, because when I do that I can feel my soul mate is out there. I know he is coming; he just needs to hurry up. This may sound crazy, but I feel like he and I have already met spiritually. I have never told that to anyone and am so embarrassed to admit that to you."

"Rebecca, I make my living talking to people about seeing colors and hearing voices. It is totally safe to tell me anything you are feeling and or seeing. I love your vision board idea, and it sounds beautiful. However, I want to ask you again, how do you let the physical world and your community of peers know you are looking for a relationship?"

"I don't understand."

"Are you dating?"

"No."

"Have you asked anyone out recently?"

"No way! Never. I would never do that; I'm not desperate. That is the man's role."

"Okay, have you asked your friends to set you up?"

"God, no, blind dates are the worst."

"Then, do you have an online dating profile?"

"I've downloaded a couple of dating apps, but guys on there are just looking to hook up. I really hate having to go through the awkward dating phase; it seems like such a waste of my time. I just want to be in a relationship."

Rebecca was the perfect example of someone who was ignoring red energy and her emotional landscape. Her vision board sounded lovely, but avoiding dates was preventing her from the natural process of emotionally connecting with potential soul mates. She didn't seem to have any awareness that a lack of connection at work and in her personal life was affecting her ability to attract a mate.

In addition, she was not giving the universe any kind of sign that she was, in fact, open to a relationship. Of course, it is understandable to find dating awkward. I myself know the torture of sitting through a dinner where you struggle to find things in common or come to the realization that you don't like this person. Then there is the chance you like the other person but must experience rejection when that feeling is not reciprocated. Those moments make us cringe, but this makes up a critical part of attracting a soul mate. Gauging how we feel on a bad date teaches us what feelings to look for when we are on a *good* date. This is precisely the point of red energy: to teach us how to check in with our emotions in all situations.

I hear similar stories from other clients who want to manifest romantic relationships. They can get stuck in what I call the "vision phase." They are aware that they want a partner, but they do not want to expose themselves to the learning process of dating, because it comes with vulnerable emotions. There is a safety to fantasy and daydreaming about our Prince or Princess Charming. We can be, say, and act however we want. We can negotiate and manage the emotions of other people in this dream scenario without taking the risk of being vulnerable. But taking action and letting people see our emotions through dating creates a sense of vulnerability. That's the thing about ruby red; it forces us to be completely aware of any vulnerability in our emotional field.

"So where is the vision board in your house?"

"I have it hanging on the inside of my closet door."

"Rebecca, don't you think that is interesting?"

"Why?"

"When I ask you how you are letting the world know that you want love, you say you haven't talked about it with friends or put it out there in any physical way. Your vision board is the only proof that the universe has of what you want. You designed this vision board to bring you joyful emotions and the feeling of excitement about the relationship that you are manifesting. Yet it's hidden away in your closet. What does that tell the universe?"

"Oh, well, that's because my closet is a sanctuary. It is the size of a small bedroom. I get dressed in there. It has a sofa where I like to have coffee and visualize in the morning."

"It sounds beautiful, but when we are tracking energy, we have to look at what we are doing to see if it is working. From what I can tell, you are stuck in the spiritual realm of creating more love and intimacy in your life."

"I don't agree. I feel pretty clear that I am trying to attract a relationship in this realm. I thought you would tell me it will just happen when it's supposed to happen."

"Rebecca, what I am about to say I mean with the deepest amount of respect. I do agree in a natural progression of the universe. But if no effort were required on your part, why make a vision board at all? Why do anything if it's just going to happen when it's supposed to happen?"

Rebecca was taken aback, but she agreed to try some of my suggestions before our next coaching session.

"The next step in grounding your intention is to share it with the universe, and I think red energy can help. You need to let people know that you are available for love and to honor the part of you that feels vulnerable. I wish I could tell you that just lighting a candle or making a vision board is enough to attract the love of your life. I do think a vision board can help you ground this energy, but the universe responds to action. Just as you had to go to school and study to get your law degree, we have to take physical steps to attract love."

I gently pointed out to Rebecca that by not dating, not talking to her friends or co-workers about relationships, and not creating an online profile, there was a chance no one knew she was available. In fact, her actions were more in line with telling the universe she does *not* want a relationship.

"Red energy helps us connect with our emotions and our vulnerability. Who do you currently feel the safest with in your life?"

"My sister, Allison," she quickly replied.

"Perfect. This week I want you to try different ways of activating ruby red energy, with the intention of helping you access your emotions. I know it may not seem related to finding love, but I just want you to try this out and see how it goes. I want you to talk to Allison in terms of your emotions and share whether you are feeling happy, sad, or angry, as well as the reasons why. Then I want you to proudly show her your vision board."

"Okay, I'll try. But she will think I'm crazy, because I've never done that with her before."

"Who cares? This is just an experiment. And if you feel vulnerable about showing her the vision board, change the language and call it a goal board."

I explained the process of activating red energy and how Rebecca could use it to connect with her emotions. I advised her to surround herself with red through daily visualization. For a universal activation, she was going to buy herself red roses and place them in the center of her house. They could have been any red flower, but based on the description of her closet, it felt like roses weren't out of the budget!

"The reason we are placing roses in your house is to have a visual reminder you are allowing people to see your heart's desire."

I wanted Rebecca to activate red in her home and throughout her day to see where she might be blocking emotional intimacy without knowing it. During the following session, I checked in on her progress.

"I decided to take your advice. The flower part was easy, and I really enjoyed the visualization of red. I tried to really keep an eye on my emotions to see how I was feeling during the week. Work was interesting for me because I did not realize how much I've been censoring my feelings there. My office is a pretty corporate environment where expressing emotion is not exactly encouraged. I've become comfortable operating from a pragmatic standpoint—maybe too comfortable. Talking to my sister was the most awkward because I've never been that honest with her about my feelings before. But I think I learned the most there. I invited her over for dinner and shared my vision board with her. At first, she joked with me and called it my love Ouija board. But then, after a few glasses of wine, we got to talking seriously."

"Sounds like you activated some red wine as well! How did it go?"

"It was really surprising. She had no idea I wanted to be in a relationship. I guess I assumed she would know since we talk regularly, even though I never specifically told her about that. She said my personality can come off as standoffish with new people, and that I have been that way since we were kids. I told her about my work with you and asked if I could do a spiritual activation with her."

"What happened?"

"Well, it brought up some major feelings for me. Love is a sensitive topic for me because I really do want to be in a relationship, and it feels like an area where I have failed. My sister figured I didn't want to talk about it, and she was right. I never really dated when I was younger, and she just assumed I was at an age where people should stop asking if I was in a relationship. It just made me sad, and I started crying. I don't think I've done that in front of her, or anyone, since I was a little kid."

"I know that may have felt scary, Rebecca, but this is really good. You are accessing your emotions in a powerful way. Tell me more."

"We had such a great night talking about my fears of dating, and she told me silly stories about when she and her husband first met. It may have been the wine talking, but we ended up joining a matchmaking service and she helped me create a profile. I still don't like the idea of blind dates, but Allison suggested I think of it as having my dates curated for me. That doesn't seem so bad."

I was so proud of Rebecca. The energy of ruby red was already helping her access her heart. I didn't think she would necessarily meet the love of her life on her first few dates through a matchmaker, but she needed to go out with a few people to open her relationship with her inner emotions. We laughed that her sister didn't believe in vision boards or any of "this New Agey stuff," but this is a perfect example of red energy helping us get in tune with our feelings. You can access energy and emotional information like this in any way that you like.

Rebecca's activation of red improved her relationship with her sister and also the relationship she had with herself. When she took an honest look at herself, she saw she needed to show her personality and start emoting more. I believe this will ultimately guide Rebecca to the loving relationship she is looking for. I personally think ruby red helps our vibration shift on an energetic level—but hey, I'm New Agey like that.

ACTIVATING RUBY RED NOTES

DO I HAVE A HEALTHY RELATIONSHIP WITH MY EMOTIONS?

If feelings are your go-to place, like they are for me, then this color will prompt you to examine whether any of your relationships are emotionally draining and how to manage that. For those of us that feel deeply, we tend to "overgive" and overshare. At a dinner party, I am the one who can't help but steer the conversation toward something deep. Someone may ask me to pass the brussels sprouts, and before I've handed them over, we're already in the middle of an existential conversation about the meaning of life. This is my comfort zone, and it is not always fair to put other people in that situation. Ruby red helps us find that balance.

One time, I met a friend and her new boyfriend at a restaurant. She excused herself to go to the bathroom, and by the time she returned, he had confessed his father had murdered his mother and was in jail for life. We were both welling up with tears, while my friend looked at me with an expression that said, "Really, Dougall—again?" I just can't help it; I want to connect on an emotional level, and I think people respond to that. Ruby red has taught me how to manage that energy. The truth is, not everyone wants to go that deep all the time, and it can be emotionally taxing for me as well. Ruby red helps me access my heart energy when I need it, but also shows me how to protect myself if I am using it as an escape.

With ruby red, you want to pay close attention to your heart center and how your emotions are affecting your experience. Ruby red naturally touches every part of the human body, as it is directly associated with the heart. After any ruby red activation, you may want to try placing your hand over your heart and taking some deep breaths. It is important to make physical contact with your heart center because it will help you connect with your emotional body. The heart is one of the very few organs we can actually *feel*, since it beats and circulates our blood. As you are activating this emotional color, touch your heart and send it loving-kindness. Check in with your heart as you activate your emotional connection. Emotional balance is one of the most important aspects of living a happy life.

SPIRITUAL ACTIVATION NOTES

We live in a society geared toward looking outside of ourselves for answers, validation, and connection. Various experts tell us everything we need to do so we can maintain our health, our homes, and our lives. Between television and social media, it is easy to start comparing our lives to or getting energy from the lives of others. Rarely do we check in with our inner expert, ourselves. For example, think of your day yesterday. How many times did you really check in with yourself emotionally to see how you felt? Now think about how many times you checked in with the outside world or with someone else. Facebook, the news, or texting a friend or family member—even reading gossip about a stranger's life in a magazine or website—probably came before getting a status update on your own well-being. These are all forms of being pulled away from your emotional center.

Jody was a client of mine who used spiritual activation as a way to balance ruby red energy in her life. She was a real estate agent on Long Island who had been in business with her younger sister, Stephanie, for years. They alternated hosting open houses and created a nice business while sharing the work. It was a great idea at the start, but lately Jody had been feeling stressed and on edge at work. She had a sensitive, empathic energy, and it seemed like her relationship with red was beginning to veer toward the shadow side. I thought she should try spiritually activating ruby red through meditation and journal her feelings as a way to get in touch with her emotions.

Jody and Stephanie were very close, but had quite different personalities. Jody was a shy, laid-back type, while Stephanie was more outgoing and motivated. Stephanie also tended to make many of their decisions, and Jody just went along with them. The idea of going into business together was Stephanie's, and it seemed like a convenient way for them to split the amount of work. But when Jody had children, she realized she wanted to stay home full time. As we spoke, I kept seeing my sister, Tarrin, with whom I am very close, in my mind.

"Jody, if you want to stop working, then why don't you?"

"I can't. Things are really busy right now, and my sister needs me. I don't want to hurt her feelings."

I felt that, as a sensitive person, Jody needed to find emotional balance with her sister. I asked her to spiritually activate red and keep notes on how she was feeling until our next session. Since she worked so much, I suggested she set a reminder on her phone to do this (see the exercise below). When we spoke next, I was eager to find out how it went.

"Boy, Dougall, every time my phone would remind me to ask 'how do you feel?' my answer would be 'stressed,' or some version of that emotion. I usually felt hurried, overwhelmed, or annoyed on my way to show a house. I love my job and know I am blessed, but I miss my kids and want to be at home with them."

Keeping regular notes on her emotional state helped Jody see that she had been going along with her sister's decisions since they were kids. Although that had been fine for many years, it was time for Jody to explain her needs so she could balance the emotional exchange with Stephanie. She was just not used to asking for what she needed.

Stephanie was understanding and agreed Jody should have more time at home. She asked for a compromise and they hired another agent so Jody could take a full year off. This way, Jody could come back to work if she wanted to, but there was not any pressure. Activating ruby red helped her balance the emotional exchange with her sister so she could have the time she wanted with her kids.

SPIRITUAL ACTIVATION EXERCISE: HOW DO I FEEL?

1. For this exercise, set a reminder on your phone to ask yourself three times a day how you feel. This may seem silly, but just humor me. There is great wisdom in making it a habit to assess your emotions.

2. You will be describing your emotional state, in writing, after spiritually activating red. Since you will be doing this in the midst of your day, it is fine to make the spiritual activation brief. Just make sure that you visualize ruby red and ground it through your entire body before answering the question. Keep a log of your answers in a journal, or just write them in your phone notes if you like. Try to begin each sentence with "I feel" in order to keep the emphasis on gauging your emotions. Here are a couple of examples:

- 9 A.M.: I feel inspired at work because I got up early to go for a run. Exercise makes me feel good—why don't I do that more?

- 2 P.M.: I feel kind of guilty for not inviting the new assistant to lunch. I wanted to just sit quietly and read, but I also know how it feels not to know anybody. I will invite her to lunch with me tomorrow so she feels welcomed.

- 10 P.M.: I feel happy! I met up with Andrea for tea, and it was so nice to catch up. I kind of wanted to go home and watch TV, but we haven't seen each other in months and I am so glad we got together.

3. Place an emphasis on your emotional reactions to various situations. As you check in with yourself, make sure you continue to spiritually activate ruby red. This will help you pay accurate attention to the range of emotions that may come up. What area of life do they fall into?

It's best to do this exercise for a week, but three days would be the minimum. You may notice the trend that there are some areas of your life where you aren't as happy as you thought. You may also connect with some really deep joy you may not have been fully embracing.

UNIVERSAL ACTIVATION NOTES (AKA "I SPY" WITH MY INTUITIVE EYE)

When is the last time you were fully honest about how you felt? Have you ever felt like your response to certain questions has become robotic? For many of us, "How are you?" is not so much a question as it is just a greeting. A friend may ask how you are, and before you even think, your response might be, "Fine, thanks." It's like it rolls off your tongue before you even consider the question. Is there a chance you may be creating an illusion? I do believe there are only a select few beings in our lives we feel comfortable enough with to disclose what's going on in our emotional lives.

Anytime you see red during this activation, it is a reminder to connect with your heart and emotional wellness. What I love about ruby red is how easily you can connect with this energy just by placing your hand over your heart. When you acknowledge this color in your day, take a moment to place your hand over your heart and take a few breaths. Feel the power and strength of that heart muscle. It is quite literally bringing life to every cell in your being. You are alive, connected, and a deeply feeling person.

UNIVERSAL ACTIVATION EXERCISE: SHARING OUR FEELINGS

This particular exercise will help you ground your emotions by entrusting them to someone else.

Find an appropriate time to honestly share your feelings with another person. When I say appropriate, I mean something like confiding in an old friend at lunch. It can be an excited, happy feeling, or perhaps a sad, negative thought you might be having. It is truly important to have a safe place to express and exercise your varied emotional states, which is the point of this exercise.

An alternative to this exercise is talk therapy. There is no shame in this, and I personally feel everyone should try it at some point in life. Therapy is such a powerful example of creating a safe environment to express your emotions. A good therapist will provide a neutral space for you to express and release any emotions that aren't serving you.

If you are anything like me, this exercise might almost be *too* easy for you.

RUBY RED AFFIRMATION

I HONOR MY EMOTIONS IN A HEALTHY WAY.

PHYSICAL ACTIVATION NOTES

If you are working on balancing your emotional exchanges, physically activating red can be a useful tool, particularly if you have a tendency to overshare like I do. Instead of a physical activation exercise, I will share a story of how I personally used red in a physical activation.

I was scheduled to do a photo shoot for a project with the ABC network. I had received an e-mail from them saying they wanted to take some photos of me for promotional purposes. Sounds fancy, right? As I drove to the address they provided, I figured that this would be a fairly small and simple affair. Feeling both excited and nervous about the opportunity, I wore red argyle socks as a physical activation.

Having my photo taken has got to be one of the most awkward things on the planet for me. I have no problem at all talking into a camera for a video, but there is something about taking still photos that makes me completely freeze. David and I were to arrive at the studio at 9 A.M. As we opened the doors and walked in, I blanched. To our right was an enormous set that appeared to be the size of an airplane hangar. At least 20 people milled about, carrying clipboards and moving equipment. In the center of the room was a stage with a raised black platform and a stark white background. Opposite the stage was a series of lights that were each about as big as a midsize car. They were not playing around here. ABC had an entire day of photos scheduled for various on-camera hosts, and, as a result, it was a very large production. I picked my jaw up off the floor and was quickly escorted into hair and makeup.

After coming out of the makeup room, I was feeling a tad more confident. Good makeup and hair people are amazing at building self-esteem in their clients, and they were so sweet to me. I decided to walk up and quickly introduce myself to the photographer, who was sitting at the foot of the stage adjusting his camera. He seemed busy, but I figured it couldn't hurt to bond with him. He sort of looked like a Santa Claus who'd had enough of being jolly and decided to join a biker gang instead.

"Hi, I'm Dougall. I'm a nervous wreck, and my first look will be 'deer in the headlights.'" I thought this would be a light joke that might break the ice and also make it clear I was apprehensive about having my photo taken. The photographer stared at me for a beat, shook my hand, and looked back down at his camera. His assistant, who was nearby, asked me to step up onto the black platform and directed me where to stand. Music played in the background as the car-sized lights shined into my eyes. Another assistant to my left offered me water, and I took it, hoping that I might be able to connect with him and feel safe in the moment.

"Man, I hate this stuff. I feel like a nervous wreck up here."

This comment again was met with silence, but this time the assistant glared at me and walked away. On second thought, this might not be the best moment to, say, offer everyone one of David's homemade blueberry muffins. I took a deep breath and could feel that my emotions were running too high. I looked down at my red argyle socks and touched them. (Colorful socks are one of my favorite ways to incorporate color energy through physical activation.) Whenever I touch them, I visualize myself absorbing ruby red energy.

I was looking for outside connection, but I needed to look inward. In truth, I was here to do a job, and so was everyone else. My nerves were causing me to overshare because I was looking for emotional validation. They had at least five more people who needed their photos taken before they could break for lunch, and the team just wanted to finish their work.

I could also feel the unspoken message that someone else in that room would have loved to be up on that stage having their photo taken. I realized my insecurity may have come across as ungrateful complaining. As I touched my red socks, my intention was to remind myself of ruby red. I honor my emotions, but this was not the time to share. Later, I would share the experience with a member of my soul group, when it was safe.

I took my hands off my socks and did my best to channel confidence. More importantly, I tried to laugh and just enjoy the moment. I don't take myself too seriously, so laughing helped me make it fun for myself. At one point, I needed to walk "like I mean it" from one end of the stage to the other. I mustered up everything that I learned from watching years of *America's Next Top Model* and *Project Runway*. I smized and served face; Tyra Banks would have been proud.

Later that day, I called my sister, Tarrin, to relay the truth of how I really felt. It was a safe place for me to talk about the pimple on my cheek, the part of me that didn't feel good enough to be there, and the fear I experienced.

My red socks reminded me not only to acknowledge my feelings, but also to put them in perspective.

Physically activating red helps us focus on our emotional self-care. I recommend activating ruby red through a color prop and keeping notes on how you respond to an influx of its energy. Do you feel more emotional than usual? Does it bring up emotions that are enjoyable or uncomfortable? Either way, developing quicker ways of gauging your emotional states will help you manage your needs in the long run.

Some red color props you could incorporate into your day include:

- **Red apples or cherries.** I love physically activating red fruit as I eat it. Red fruits can also be displayed in a bowl as a visual, touchable reminder.

- **Cosmetics.** Red lips or nails are a fun way to incorporate red energy throughout your day.

- **Red socks.** Just like I did while having my photo taken, you can use red socks as a color prop to check in with your emotions at any time.

This is also a great time to go through old photos in an effort to stir up romantic or nostalgic feelings. Take a photo of a happy time or moment in your life. Then take a red piece of paper and paste the image on it. Looking at this image surrounded by red will help maximize your connection to your emotional center.

THE SHADOW SIDE OF RUBY RED

The shadow side of ruby red is usually represented by being oversensitive. But it can also show up as seeming insensitive or disconnected. Ruby red is about developing communication with our moods and emotional levels. If you find you have moments of leaning too far in either direction, you're not alone. In fact, it is very common to have times in our lives when we experience the shadow side of red. Feelings are a very intangible thing for many people, and we are constantly presented with situations that may trigger emotional reactions.

The shadow side of red is a reminder for you to gauge your emotions and make the adjustments that will help your heart feel balanced. You might need to pull back emotionally on occasion. Sometimes what is considered "needy" is your desire for emotional validation. In this case, red will help you acknowledge if you are ignoring your innate emotional intelligence. Balancing red energy will also help you carve out space in your life to ensure you have the opportunity to connect with your emotions and get things off your chest, so to speak. Allow ruby red to guide you in finding those opportunities.

If you are feeling disconnected, I find that watching an emotionally charged movie is a good way to help activate emotional energy as well.

CHAPTER 9

❖

ORANGE

QUALITIES: Balance and perception
SHADOW SIDE: Uneven, scattered energy

Orange is an excellent color to activate during busy or hectic times. When we are in the thick of any big undertaking, we may neglect certain elements of ourselves as we put all our focus on the goal. This is completely natural when striving to achieve anything. But in the process, it can become difficult to find perspective. Whether we are motivated toward something specific or just feeling frazzled by life, orange helps us to bring the imbalanced aspects of our consciousness into equilibrium. In doing so, orange also helps us bring our intuitive sense to its highest possible level. For me, orange feels like a quiet meditation room with essential oils wafting through the air and soft music playing; it just feels good. If you feel scattered or overextended in your life, look no further than orange.

Buddhism has some of the strongest associations with the color orange, as seen by the orange robes that Buddhist monks wear. Buddhists consider orange to be the color of spiritual radiance, which is the point when our souls reach the highest state of evolution. I love this symbolic imagery because I often feel like my energy radiates warmth when I activate orange. The balancing orange color of the monks' robes is said to have been chosen by Buddha himself, in the 5th century B.C.E. Other religions that value the color orange include Hinduism and Protestantism.

Confucianism (the main religion of ancient China) considered orange to be the color of metamorphosis and renewal. According to this philosophy, our life's journey is determined by whether or not we can find balance between the yin (female) and yang (male) energy that exists inside all of us. Orange is the color that helps us reconcile our inner imbalance so we can find a state of harmony.

In the art world, orange is incredibly popular when paired with opposing colors. In fact, artist Claude Monet inspired the entire impressionist movement with his painting *Impression, Sunrise*, which showcased a (then) unusual placement of the radiant orange sun reflecting against blue clouds and water. Students of color theory know that orange and blue are opposite colors, meaning that both colors become more vivid when you place them next to each other on a canvas. This is a perfect representation of orange, because working with it will brighten every other area of your life. Just like in a painting, using orange not only highlights every other color it is near, but it also balances their energies as well. The beauty of orange in your life will stabilize everything that it is near.

Visually, orange is the easiest color to perceive on land or water, particularly in darker lighting. For this reason, it is the color of choice for life rafts, life jackets, and construction signs. Astronaut uniforms are usually orange due to the fact they are the easiest to be perceived in space. Highway workers tend to wear orange because it helps them to be easily seen. I like to use orange because it serves as my beacon for heightened perception.

Orange represents balance of all things, and, most importantly, it highlights the balance between psychology and spirituality. Some of my spiritual teachers have said it is the color of psychic abilities or intuition, which may explain my attraction to it. Intuition, at its finest, is most accurate when the various elements of our lives are balanced. This was something I didn't come to understand for quite some time.

I used to think being psychic was the highest form of spiritual connection, but I now know this isn't necessarily true. Obsessing over any aspect of our life, whether it's our job or anything else, will by definition cause us to neglect other areas. I believe intuition is the by-product of meditation and finding emotional as well as spiritual balance. We can be highly psychic and perceive accurate information about someone else's life, but true intuitive wisdom comes from finding balance in the various areas of our own lives.

When I first started connecting with energy, being psychic was my main focus. I was laser-focused on being a good clairvoyant for others, but I had emotional blinders on as to what it meant to actually live in a state of peace, joy, and connection. I was training my psychic muscle, and it was certainly growing, but I could feel when I started to plateau. Not only did I plateau, but my soul and emotional body also began to feel tired. I used to get headaches after working with clients. I had no idea how to manage my energy and not a clue that my issues were stemming from neglecting my own physical body as well as my emotional being.

That's the ironic part about self-care. Sensitive people often put the needs of other people before their own needs. But the more we look inward and do the necessary work to improve ourselves, the better able we are to use our intuition for others. My career started in Dallas, Texas, when I was in my late teens. At the time, I would get hired for private parties around the area. It felt like such a gift from the universe at that age. I would be paid somewhere around $100 an hour, and I could spend the whole evening at a party with my little card table set up. I would give back-to-back readings with no break.

On one particular night, I was at a birthday party for a woman in a charming suburb outside of Dallas.

"Dougall, this was so wonderful. Thank you for making such an exciting party," Sheila said.

I liked Sheila. She really honored what I did, whereas at other parties, I sometimes ended up feeling like a juggling monkey. People would laugh about the "fortune teller" in the corner, and I would sit by myself for hours as they socialized with each other. I would polish my crystals or shuffle my tarot cards, waiting for someone to walk over and ask for a reading. But Sheila was quite kind and always made me feel comfortable.

"Why don't you stay and have something to eat?" she asked.

"Oh, no, I'm fine. I need to leave to disconnect from the energy."

This was partially true. During events, or when I had done small parties in the past, when the readings were done, I usually wanted to leave. It was a lot of energy to give out, and to suddenly jump into just chatting socially was a little challenging for me. The other reality at that time was I didn't like public eating. I had not come out yet and was really struggling with shame about my weight at that point. If I were in a restaurant, at someone's home, or really anywhere in public, I would eat like a bird (albeit a very small bird with body image issues). This must have been startling, because at the time I was six feet six and about 300 pounds. So clearly I was eating somewhere. Instead of facing this issue head-on, I convinced myself food got in the way of reading energy properly. That sounds pretty balanced, right?

I politely excused myself from Sheila's party. I gave as spiritual a good-bye as I thought a psychic should. I would say a quick blessing and some namastes, all the while fantasizing about the pizza I would have at home. I hopped into my turquoise Jetta convertible and pulled out of her driveway. I was not taking care of myself emotionally or physically, and this imbalance was affecting me. As I rounded the corner, I recall feeling a little scattered, and the next thing I knew I was jolted by a collision with another car.

"What the—?" I said as I opened the door of my turquoise chariot.

My energy was all askew, and I got out of the car, walking toward the man who so rudely hit me.

"This is a one-way street," he calmly said.

"It is?" I said.

"You were going the wrong direction on a one-way street."

My eyes started welling up with tears. I can only describe this stranger as a father figure. I immediately knew he had children. His kids weren't in the car, but he could tell I was out of it, the way that a parent can.

Being a gay psychic in the suburbs of Texas, at that time in particular, did not feel completely safe. There were definitely people in that area who, because of religion or for whatever reason, had some major judgment of me. Not only that, but I had just hit someone while driving a turquoise car with a pop-up sign in my backseat that said "Psychic, channel, and card reader" in huge letters. This may not have been the best moment for me to start crying, but that's exactly what happened.

"I don't have car insurance," was all I could utter.

"Okay, okay, calm down; take a deep breath," he said. "How old are you?"

"I'm 19."

At 19, having car insurance was a huge financial commitment for me. It was my first year of flying solo, meaning I had moved out on my own and no longer got any help from my family. At this point in my life, I hadn't a clue about how to organize my finances, and making a $600 monthly payment for something I "might" use seemed like a perfectly reasonable expense to avoid.

This is one of those life moments where I feel so lucky things turned out the way that they did. I was so scattered it didn't even occur to me to ask this man if he was okay or hurt at all. Instead, he kindly said we could come up with a plan. We exchanged information, and in the following week, we arranged a payment plan. We did not call the police, and no insurance companies were involved. He placed so much trust in me that I was absolutely determined to pay him for the damage, which I did.

That accident was a wake-up call on so many levels. I realized I was hiding behind these spiritual illusions. I was spending so much time accessing psychic energy that the other areas of my life were totally out of balance. My finances were in disarray, I was completely neglecting my physical health, and now my actions were potentially harming others. Something had to change.

When I began activating orange, it highlighted my need for balance in areas where I was neglecting myself. I had been seeing this color around people who were very balanced, which was a quality I wanted more of. With this in mind,

I experimented with activating it myself. Like a magnet, it would draw a desire out of me to know and search out other aspects of my consciousness.

I decided to regularly use orange as my divine compass to help me find a state of spiritual equilibrium. Oddly, the payments I made for the fender bender ended up becoming a regular reminder that I needed take better care of myself. In the beginning, I made small changes. I started walking outside for 15 minutes a day and began paying closer attention to my food choices. Instead of starving myself before a reading and then overeating junk food later, I tried to eat a reasonable portion of fresh food. Consuming healthy food did make me feel better, but I didn't become vegan or only eat raw foods. Rather than making drastic changes, I allowed balance to be elevated to the forefront of my consciousness.

It's important to know that one area of your life may be dominant in certain moments, and that is okay. For example, imagine you have just fallen in love. The friends you have been spending so much time with will suddenly take a backseat in your priorities. You will probably invest extra time in this budding relationship. You may play hooky from work or take the day off from school as your two souls bond together. Part of this process involves retreating somewhat from the outside world. As time passes, the foundation of the relationship begins to strengthen and grow. Once you have integrated, you will realize it's time to reconnect with your friends, your work, or your family. You cannot stay in hibernation mode forever, or the other areas of your life will fall out of balance.

Just as in new love, this principle applies to your career. Let's say you are very motivated at work, and you have just been promoted. That surge of positive energy will cause you to place even more focus on your job, setting it above everything else. Your friends and family hopefully support your hard work and will take joy in watching you give it your all. But if you ignore all other aspects of your life, this will begin to take a toll on your relationships.

The orange light teaches us that yes, we can have one area of our life lead us and temporarily take precedence. But to achieve the kind of balance that brings about true perception, we must recenter ourselves and maintain a level of engagement with the rest of our lives.

ACTIVATING ORANGE NOTES

WHAT ELEMENTS OF MY LIFE ARE OUT OF BALANCE?

Activating orange is usually an easy and natural progression, since it is the combination of psychology and spirituality. With ruby red, our focus was on accessing the emotional body. But with orange, we are accessing a level that is deeper than our emotions, and that is our intuition. Intuition is a by-product of meditation and healthy spiritual practice, and it is also the result of living in balance. The more our lives are in harmony, the easier it is for us to intuit the best choices in our life.

Please note, some students have reported slight dizziness as they activate orange. Personally, I think this is a result of feeling every part of our being on a more intimate level. Orange will help us connect with the physical, emotional, and spiritual parts of our consciousness. Not only that, but it also allows us to see and feel how these areas are all co-existing.

SPIRITUAL ACTIVATION NOTES

Balance is a pretty broad term, and I don't think any of us live in a constant state of balance. As we each take our respective journeys through life, we face different issues that bring various aspects of our energy to the surface. We have moments when one portion of our life requires more attention than the others, but the balancing act is all about *not* dropping the ball with respect to the other areas of our lives. In order to be fully integrated beings, we must be engaged with all aspects of our life.

The orange light helps us check in with every aspect of our consciousness, providing a deep reflection of it as we activate this color energy. With each color we use, we magnify a part of our being. From enabling practical thoughts with gold, to connecting our heart and emotions with ruby, we turn the volume up on whichever energy we want to harness. Orange gives us the opportunity to take a bird's-eye view of our lives, to give us perspective on how all these parts are interacting together.

SPIRITUAL ACTIVATION EXERCISE: DESIGN THE IDEAL DAY

My favorite part of using orange in a spiritual activation is that it requires us to slow down and do a form of meditation. Since orange helps us find balance, spiritual activation is a particularly useful activity. When we close our eyes to ground orange energy through our body, it is naturally balancing and soothing.

This exercise with orange will help us balance and manage our energy. We have all had that ideal day where everything just seems to go the way we want, and our goal here is to design that day from the ground up. Orange energy is not about experiencing the height of ecstasy in our lives. It is about attaining a happy, Zen medium.

The ideal day isn't when you win the lottery, your wedding day, or the day your kids were born. These are incredible, magical experiences, but they also result in huge spikes of adrenaline and energy. They are once-in-a-lifetime events. The ideal orange day is a balanced, enjoyable, routine day that reflects your life where it is now. For example, your ideal day should not include sunset yoga by the beach if you live nowhere near the ocean and have to pick the kids up from school at 4 P.M.

My ideal day always starts with a hot cup of coffee and some morning alone time. Even if I have to leave the house at five in the morning, I will get up an hour before that to be quiet and connect with myself. Quiet time in the morning is sacred and important to my sense of balance. If you are the type of person who jumps out of bed in the morning, your perfect day might start with something productive, like an early walk.

1. Envision your perfect day. After spiritually activating orange, your goal for this exercise is to calm and refocus your energy so you can visualize this day from a balanced spiritual place. Take your time in grounding orange energy through your body before you map out your day. In times of stress, it may be difficult to remind yourself what is really important and where you need to make more effort. Spiritually activating orange simplifies the task of seeing what makes up a satisfying day for you.

2. List the details of your perfect day on a piece of paper. To help you in this exercise, look at the average kind of day you currently experience. What is working and what is not? If there are elements you feel are missing, incorporate them into your perfect day. This should be the

kind of day that feels balanced and happy for you. Would it start with cuddling with your dog in bed? Or perhaps you would do some gardening in the backyard. This should be the kind of day you would be happy to live over and over. For example, you might wake up early to reflect and watch the sunrise. You would have enough time to connect with yourself (perhaps through meditation) and prepare for your day. Your hair would do everything you want it to, and your favorite shirt would fit perfectly. At your job, you would feel honored by your co-workers and creatively inspired. By the time you crawl into bed, you would have a sense of accomplishment, peace, and contentment. Again, the specifics of this day are up to you and what you need to attain balance.

3. Commit to incorporating at least one item from your perfect day into your current life. Keep your list handy, and remind yourself of your perfect day anytime you activate orange.

Note: Take your time scripting your day out. The key word you are looking for is *balance*. Think of your life as a meal. If you focus too much attention on one part of the meal, it may feel disproportionate. You could whip up the most amazing homemade cranberry sauce, but you ultimately would feel unsatisfied if that were the only thing on the plate.

UNIVERSAL ACTIVATION NOTES (AKA "I SPY" WITH MY INTUITIVE EYE)

Orange is one of my favorite colors to pull energy from in autumn, from beautiful orange leaves to pumpkins on every doorstep. On any given morning, the sun rises and includes shades of warm orange. And with each sunset, I am again reminded of the timeless balance of orange. When you see orange, no matter where you are, ask yourself:

- Where is there imbalance in my life?

- Do I feel in alignment with my center? Am I spreading my attention over the areas that make my life feel whole and complete? Or is one thing taking up too much energy?

Just as in the story of how too many readings and not eating well resulted in my fender bender, when we are out of balance, the universe will remind us to take care of ourselves.

UNIVERSAL ACTIVATION EXERCISE: LIVING IN THE WEEK

In the self-help world, we are often told we must strive to live in the present moment. Living in the moment sounds great in theory, but I'd really like to speak to someone who actually lives in the moment on a constant basis. From what I've seen with my clients, most of us are either focused on the future or trying to learn from the past, and staying in the present is quite difficult. Orange will help us to see how present we are in any given moment.

I have a new mantra, and it is that I live *in the week*. Perhaps it is because my job involves looking into the future, but

I find myself constantly thinking ahead. Still, I know being present is important to a sense of balance. Living in the week allows me to acknowledge what is on the short-term horizon, which in turn helps me to be more present.

Anytime you see orange, this is the universe's way of asking how present you are in that moment. Allow the universal activation of orange energy to show you where you could be more present. Do one thing on that same day that will help bring your consciousness fully into the present moment. Physical activities are often helpful for grounding yourself in the present moment. These could include any kind of exercise such as a hike. Mindfulness meditation is also very useful for staying in the present moment.

If I can live in the week, then I feel like a spiritual rock star. Operating in a span of seven days helps me to find my balance. Maybe I missed the gym or meditation on Tuesday, but I can catch up by going on Wednesday. No big deal. Perhaps there is one day I am very focused on writing, but then the next day David and I play hooky so we can have a family day. The idea I am trying to get across is about finding balance. Just like most of us, I have a family, job, friends, hobbies, and a variety of other aspects of my life that I juggle. Living in the moment may not be on the agenda today, and that is okay. Once you compare your perfect day to your average day, you can start making adjustments to find more balanced contentment.

ORANGE AFFIRMATION

I HAVE BALANCED, INTUITIVE ENERGY.

PHYSICAL ACTIVATION NOTES

Physical activations are very helpful during stressful or hectic times, because touching an orange color prop has the added effect of grounding us into the present moment. It is easier to stay present when we physically engage with something in that moment. Sometimes after a full day of readings, processing a number of people, I like to rebalance my energy. One technique I use is to touch something in my office and then say what it is out loud. For example, I might touch the orange vase on my desk and say, "This is a vase." This is a very simple technique of grounding into present consciousness with my physical body.

Some other orange color props you could incorporate into your day include:

- **Dried leaves.** I personally love the colors of autumn and the various shades of orange that can be observed in nature. To bring some of this energy into your home, collect orange leaves and dry them so you can display them all year long.

- **Turmeric.** Both dried and fresh turmeric possess a vibrant shade of orange that can be incorporated into your meals. Aside from providing balancing orange energy, turmeric is also excellent for reducing all kinds of inflammation and restoring balance to your immune system.

- **Oranges.** When I am working with orange energy, one of my favorite color props is a bag of fresh oranges or tangelos. I keep them in my living room or kitchen in a bowl. Not only are they a visual reminder of this balancing energy, but touching them releases their invigorating scent. For me, the scent of orange brings another sense into the usage of orange as a color prop. I also like to diffuse orange and ylang-ylang essential oil as a relaxing reminder to focus on balance. The color orange not only becomes a trigger to prioritize balance, but the scent also creates a clean and fresh feeling of order in my home.

- **Carrots.** Aside from being a healthy snack, carrots possess one of the most vibrant shades of orange in nature.

PHYSICAL ACTIVATION EXERCISE: AUTUMN LEAVES

Although my favorite way to do this exercise is when the leaves change color in the fall season, there are many ways to activate orange through nature.

1. Find an outdoor spot where you can explore the beauty of nature. Possible places could include a forest or park. Set an intention to center your energy as you walk around, invoking the power of orange.

2. Try to find something orange to take home with you. Examples could include rocks, wood, or leaves. If you live in an area where the leaves change color, you have an incredible opportunity to collect some gorgeous orange foliage. If you do find something, give thanks

to the universe for affirming this orange energy within your spirit.

3. Other ways to enjoy this exercise would be:

    •   Bring an orange color prop with you, and touch it as you walk around in nature.

    •   If you see something orange but do not want to take it home, you can take a photo as a reminder of how that balanced energy brings such beauty to your environment.

THE SHADOW SIDE OF ORANGE

The shadow side of orange is witnessed in uneven or scattered energy. This will result in issues like struggling to be on time for appointments. You may have difficulty finding where you have left things in your home or workspace. If you find you lean toward the shadow side of orange, outlining your ideal day will serve as a valuable map to unlock your inner balance and heighten your perception. If you have scattered or uneven energy, some element of your life is taking too much of your focus. You may be overcommitted to something or not fully committed to honoring your center.

As you activate the orange light, you will first be identifying what area of your life is currently in the steering position. Be aware that if you are struggling with the shadow side of orange, you may feel overwhelmed, without the time to create the balance that you need. However, I find this is the mind's way of keeping us stuck in scattered energy. Even the busiest person has some expendable time during the day that could be used to balance their energy. If you watch TV or spend free time on your smartphone, then you have time to balance other elements of your life.

There is no judgment in this awareness. In a session, I often describe a phase someone is in. A career phase, a relationship phase, a family phase, or a self-care phase. Whichever one you identify with is currently steering your thoughts and is the mainstay of your energy level. As you expand and work with orange, it reminds you to also tend to the other parts of your life and to engage with everything in order to create a sense of balance and happiness.

CHAPTER 10

❖

PINK

QUALITIES: Perfection and unconditional love
SHADOW SIDE: Self-criticism; judgment of others

A salve for the self-critical, radiant pink light is the embodiment of perfection and unconditional love. Pink exudes a warm, loving energy, often seen around newborns. If you've ever held a sleeping baby, you were probably calmed by their peaceful pink energy. This is because newborns have not yet learned any of the limiting thoughts and beliefs so many of us pick up as we live our lives. As you will see, it is possible to return to a simpler, less critical frame of mind. Working with pink helps us see ourselves the way that God or the universe has created us: perfect.

Pink's association with loving energy can be observed in both scientific and intuitive ways. In home design, feng shui specifically utilizes pink due to its gentle and soothing effect on our behavior. Feng shui practitioners also place pink in the southwest area of a home, as both are connected to the energy of love and marriage. In nature, pink is one of the most common colors of flowers. Its color serves to attract insects and birds that nurture plants through pollination, and pink has also been shown to deter predators. Even the birds and the bees have a natural attraction to the warm, loving energy of pink! It has been my intuitive experience that pink helps us manifest more loving energy.

Through numerous studies in Europe and the United States, pink has been widely shown to be associated with being polite, nurturing, loving, and romantic. We see scientific validation of pink's power in a fascinating experiment by Dr. Alexander Schauss, Ph.D., director of the American Institute for Biosocial and Medical Research in Tacoma, Washington. Dr. Schauss studied the impact of color on blood pressure and pulse rate, and he wondered if a specific shade of pink could have the power to change behavior in violent criminals. He studied what would happen if the interior walls of specific jail cells at a naval correctional facility were painted what was called Baker-Miller pink. The goal was to discover how prisoners would react, and the results were startling. Aggressive outbursts and violent behavior reportedly declined markedly in response to this warm, nurturing color.[6] Other research determined pink's soothing effects on biometric response and behavior could be achieved with just 15 minutes of exposure.[7]

Pink came to me at a time in my life when I was feeling especially self-critical. I struggled with my weight as a teen and was almost 100 pounds overweight by the age of 18. Although I am not proud of my behavior in the following story, the lesson I learned has empowered me to rely on pink energy for a boost of self-love ever since.

My story with pink began on a crisp fall day in Dallas when I was twenty years old. My friend Jeremy and I hopped into my Volkswagen Cabriolet for an afternoon of lunch and shopping. Jeremy was enchanting to me. Blond, witty, and incredibly fit, he was the epitome of the Hollywood gay best friend. Jeremy dressed impeccably, always looking like he had just returned from a Ralph Lauren photo shoot. I never felt good enough when we were together and was quite critical of myself for being so out of shape compared to him.

"Ugh, I haven't worked out in at least a month!" Jeremy moaned during our lunch at Whole Foods, pinching at his completely flat abdomen.

"A month! Wow, I work out five days a week for an hour and a half with a trainer. I wish I could be as fit as you."

"Oh, that's because I've done steroids."

I practically spit out my wasabi tuna salad when he said that. It was just so cavalier! It was as if we were discussing how he got his teeth to be so white and he had said, "Oh, you like my pearly whites? It's so easy—just smoke some crack!"

I had spent two solid years losing weight the old-fashioned, natural way. I changed my eating habits. (It turns out eating egg rolls for lunch every day is not a great idea.) I was exercising and weight lifting regularly. But, as anyone who loses a lot of weight will know, you are often left with stretch marks everywhere. These days, I see stretch marks as a badge of honor, but I didn't then. Instead of congratulating myself on getting healthy, I was only focused on my "flaws," as I saw them. I could not have been any farther from pink energy and was rather steeped in its shadow side. And so, after one short conversation with a glamorous friend, I was suddenly willing to inject myself with steroids in the hope that it would make me feel confident and lovable.

I ended up paying $600 (or the equivalent of 300 egg rolls with duck sauce) for two cycles of steroids. Back at my apartment by myself, I sat on the couch, injected the syringe into my thigh, and almost immediately felt my heart sink into a shame spiral. I closed my eyes, took a few deep, cleansing breaths, and suddenly became very aware of my higher self. In my mind's eye, I saw a huge swirl of pink light around my head. It wasn't intentional in this moment, but I spiritually activated pink and grounded that energy through my body. Before I could even process what this meant, tears began to well up inside me.

What are you doing? asked a loving, nonjudgmental voice in my head. It felt like the most elevated version of my consciousness had floated to the surface.

What *was* I doing? I was at the beginning of my career of giving spiritual advice. I taught classes and workshops about integrating self-love. And yet, here I was, having one of the least unconditionally loving moments of my life. With each breath, the pink light grew bigger and brighter. I asked my higher self why I was seeing pink. The message that came through was, *You don't need to change anything; you are perfect as you are.*

In my opinion, all of us come to this planet with an innate higher self. Our higher self is the part of our being that is pure wisdom and absolute love. Think of it as the very best version of our consciousness, the part of us that is connected to the source. Daily stress, fear, and our ego can make it difficult to connect with our higher self. But when we quiet our mind through meditation, exercise, or therapeutic exercises, it becomes much easier to connect with this wisdom. Meditation in particular helps to quiet the external "noise" and allows us to receive the messages that are in our best interest. I had a meditative spiritual activation that day, and the message was loud and clear.

I grabbed the bag of syringes, walked over to the trash bin, and dropped them all in. In the following days, I reached out to my soul group for support. I made a mental note to stop looking up to Jeremy so much and to just see him as a friend who had his own set of issues to work through. I began activating pink daily to help raise my self-esteem and see what messages came through. Surrounded only by my intuition, the message of pink was perfectly clear: I am perfect *exactly as I am*. Sure, I was a work in progress and will always have room for improvement. But more than anything, I wanted to be authentically me. Ironically, those steroids ended up being possibly the best $600 I have ever spent on a life lesson.

Pink light does not magically erase our self-criticism, but it instead invites us to refocus on unconditionally loving ourselves. Instead of seeking a sense of validation from the outside world, pink teaches us to quench our thirst for acceptance by loving and validating *ourselves*. Only once we have done this will we see our true and innate perfection.

The pink lotus flower is one of the most important symbolic images in Buddhism, as it is associated with the Great Buddha himself. The pink lotus flower signifies the progression of our souls from the primitive "mud" of our ego, through the waters of evolving spirituality, and into the loving sunshine of enlightenment. This flower manages not only to survive but also to flourish in dirty, muddy conditions.

Just like the lotus flower, we do not need to try to escape the mud of our self-criticism. Instead, pink allows us to acknowledge self-criticism and shows us where we need more love in our lives. Pink benefits us by giving us a new perspective, and it allows us to fuel our growth above any further self-criticism. The truth is that most of us will always feel self-critical from time to time. Pink just turns the volume up on the kind inner voice that loves us unconditionally.

ACTIVATING PINK NOTES

AM I HONORING MY INHERENT PERFECTION?

Pink is a healing balm to help counteract the burns of our self-criticism. We live in a society that tends to promote a feeling of not being good enough, and that is why pink is so useful. Whether in the realm of physical appearance, money, social status, or career aspirations, pink helps us quiet the urge to compare ourselves critically with those around us.

We are regularly bombarded by images of airbrushed models or celebrities looking "perfect" in magazines and commercials. The explosion of social media has only made this even more pronounced and pervasive. In the modern world, we are flooded with endless opportunities to compare ourselves with others. Childhood friends, college friends, relatives, co-workers, and complete strangers are happy to flaunt their fabulous lives, or at least the version of their lives that they want you to see.

With pink light, you are called to honor and attune yourself to your own *personal* perfection. When activating pink in visualization or through the following exercises, there is no one to compare yourself to and nothing to feel bad about. It is just you, and you are exactly where you are meant to be on your journey.

Each of us is a unique expression of energy. You've heard that no two snowflakes are alike, and it is the same with soul energy. With pink, we take the time to love ourselves and recognize our individuality.

With pink, you can expect to feel an extra boost of confidence. When you meditate with pink, people may compliment you and "randomly" point out what you bring to their lives and/or to the world. *Accept those compliments.* Just say thank you and try to appreciate the love that is being directed toward you. Allow yourself to be seen and appreciated.

If you tend to be an overly self-critical person, you may notice a spike in self-criticism when you first start using pink. This is simply a clearing of negative energy. As in a juice cleanse, you may experience an unpleasant initial period as your consciousness releases toxic self-criticism. The mind spends so much time trying to refute what the soul already knows: you are perfect as you are.

SPIRITUAL ACTIVATION NOTES

Spiritually activating pink can be an emotional experience. If you have a history of being self-critical (and many of us do, to some extent), then steeping yourself in loving pink light can bring up all sorts of feelings. These run the gamut from relief, love, and happiness to resistance, anger, and regret. The brain and ego are very smart, and they will often use deceptive ways to deny us much-needed love. The goal with pink is to just allow the truth of your perfection to wash over you. You don't need to do anything to deserve love; it is your birthright.

A note on compliments: It can be easy to dismiss or reject the kind words of others out of a false sense of modesty. But this is another way for the mind to deny you love and should be avoided. If someone says something nice to you, try to really take it in and absorb what they are saying. They are sending you pink energy in that moment, and it is your decision whether or not to allow it in. Accepting compliments helps to reorient and retrain your mind toward loving yourself.

SPIRITUAL ACTIVATION EXERCISE: ACCEPT THE COMPLIMENT

For this exercise, find a close friend or relative with whom you feel safe. Explain the self-love process you are working on so they can understand your goal and serve as your supportive mirror.

1. Sit opposite your partner and do the spiritual activation process for pink with them. (It will be helpful to explain spiritual activation and how to ground pink energy through the body.)

2. When you both feel ready, ask them to specifically state their favorite qualities about you. Make sure to give them enough time to answer. Don't rush this process.

3. As they begin speaking, look them directly in the eyes and do not interrupt them. Self-criticism sometimes causes us to interrupt a compliment because we are uncomfortable with receiving love. Make sure you do not block yourself from pink energy in this way.

4. To help with this process, continue to ground pink energy throughout your physical bodies by picturing yourselves enveloped in pink as your partner speaks. Allow and intend for the pink light to fill you with a loving self-acceptance.

5. Then you must *accept the compliment.* Once they let you know they have finished answering the question, say only "Thank you." Do your best to absorb the love that has been directed at you. It can be helpful to close your eyes for a moment after they finish and do some deep breathing as you absorb the information. Allow the pink energy to fill you with love that you can use. Do not deflect the compliment or change the subject. If they love your beautiful eyes and great sense of humor, try to absorb this as deeply as you can. If they are open to it, you

can repeat this process by trading places and then complimenting them.

UNIVERSAL ACTIVATION NOTES (AKA "I SPY" WITH MY INTUITIVE EYE)

Many of us are so used to negative self-talk that we are not even conscious of doing it. Do you know whether your inner critic behaves like a snarky teenager or more like Joan "Mommie Dearest" Crawford screaming "No wire hangers!" at your inner child? Either way, you can help yourself immensely by becoming fully aware of how often these thoughts are floating around in your consciousness.

The ironic thing about negative self-talk is that we even use it to bond with other people. This is pink's shadow side sneaking into our consciousness. It is not uncommon for friends to commiserate about the things they hate in themselves in a misguided attempt at connection. If your sister says, "I hate my thighs," you do not need to criticize your own body in order to feel closer to her. It is much more powerful to harness pink energy and send it to your sister in the form of "You, and your thighs, are beautiful!"

UNIVERSAL ACTIVATION EXERCISE: TRACK YOUR PERFECTION

For those of us who struggle with self-esteem, the habit of negative self-talk is so ingrained we don't even realize we are doing it. We tend to be so much kinder to other people than we are to ourselves. But, in my experience, it is a waste of time to try to silence that inner voice because it is a part of us. I find it is much more effective to bring these thoughts into the light by consciously adding positive messages into our consciousness. In this exercise, you will harness the power of pink throughout your day by consciously infusing your consciousness with a message of self-love.

1. Set an intention that you will notice whenever pink presents itself to you throughout your day. Sometimes we miss messages from the universe because we are not able to recognize them. You can utilize a color prop as a reminder of this exercise.

2. Whenever you notice pink, take a moment to acknowledge something you did in the last few days that you are really proud of. You can do this by repeating it to yourself silently like an affirmation, or you can write it down. For example, *I have been studying diligently for my finals and am really proud of my commitment.*

3. A variation of this exercise would be to repeat the pink affirmation listed below anytime you spot pink in your life.

The point of this exercise is to redirect your critical thoughts toward more productive and positive areas of your being. The more you activate pink, the more you will get used to diluting your negative thoughts with positive ones. Once you get used to the habit of activating pink in this way, seeing it should immediately trigger a positive thought in your consciousness. This exercise will help counteract the urge to obsess over something you don't like about yourself.

Here is a very real example of this exercise in action: Weight has been my personal struggle in life, and I feel the shadow side of pink most consistently when it comes to my body image. If I am having an off day, when someone snaps a photo of me with their phone and shows me the image, my immediate thought is, *Well, look at you, you big ol' heifer!* My ego usually tries to convince me I am just being funny, but self-deprecating humor can be just as destructive as negative self-talk. This would not be a shining moment for me, but I'm just being totally real with you here. Spiritual teachers: they're just like us!

When I use this exercise, I allow pink to remind me of the positive ways in which I care for my physical health. If I go to the supermarket and see someone wearing a pink blouse, I might remind myself I am proud of exercising that morning. I might congratulate myself on the healthy dinner I was planning to make that night, or I might just use the self-love affirmation for pink. I might not be able to silence the voice that wants to criticize my body, but I can choose where to place my focus. I have managed to lose and keep off a significant amount of weight in my life, and I will not allow negative self-talk to minimize that achievement.

This approach does not focus on removing the negative thought completely. Rather, it is all about adding a dose of positive pink energy to balance and redirect the thought.

PINK AFFIRMATION

I AM PERFECT EXACTLY AS I AM.

PHYSICAL ACTIVATION NOTES

Just as a reminder, a color prop is any physical item you will use to activate the color you're working on (in this case, pink). You will want to find various pink items to remind you of pink energy every time you look at them. Once you select your items, you will infuse them with the intention of increasing your self-acceptance and unconditional love.

This is a perfect time to get creative and pick props that really inspire you! When you notice these items throughout your day, let them be a reminder of your innate perfection and self-love. I like using the following affirmation when I infuse a color prop with my intention: *Let the light be the source of the healing.* This is a reminder to remove any pressure from myself and just allow the color to do its work.

Some pink color props you could incorporate into your day include:

- **Pink nail polish.** This is an easy one if you enjoy wearing nail polish, because you will notice the color every time you look at your hands. However, feel free to adorn your body with anything pink. I often wear a pink shirt when I want to be extra loving to myself. I also notice that me wearing pink seems to make *other* people happy as well.

- **A pink pen or highlighter for notes.** For journal writing, I like to use pink ink as a visual reminder to love myself unconditionally.

- **Pink lightbulbs.** Although you wouldn't normally touch a lightbulb when it is on, I included this because it is a great way to weave color energy into your physical space. Many hardware stores sell pink lightbulbs, and using one in a lamp will bathe any room in pink energy. It also has the added benefit of making your skin look great!

PHYSICAL ACTIVATION EXERCISE: SELF-GRATITUDE JOURNAL

Keeping a gratitude journal involves listing the good things in our life that we are thankful for. With a *self*-gratitude journal, we magnify pink's positive effects by refocusing this list only on the good within ourselves. We increase the positive effects of a gratitude journal by linking those feelings to our color prop so that we can be reminded of our gratitude throughout the day.

While touching your color prop, think of something about yourself that you love and write it down in your journal. When you "pat yourself on the back," pink energy reminds you to step back and observe how far you have come. Try to be really generous with yourself here. If you have difficulty coming up with an item to list, it is a clear sign you are working through pink's shadow side. I will speak for pink here and remind you that you are lovable, valuable, and perfect *exactly as you are.*

Keep your color prop with you for the rest of the day, and remind yourself of the item on your self-gratitude list every time you touch it. The goal of this exercise is to rev up your self-love engines and get them accustomed to running at full speed. You might love your sense of humor and artistic ability, or perhaps it's something as simple as having a great hair day! With the pink light, you are empowered to honor and attune yourself to your own one-of-a-kind perfection.

Here are some questions to help with this exercise, but feel free to list whatever comes to you. Ask yourself:

- What parts of myself am I most happy with?
- What areas of my life are prospering?
- What makes me special?

- What am I talented at doing?

- What can I offer the planet?

- Am I compassionate? Do I have a knack for making others feel good?

Remember, the shadow side of pink may try to prevent you from honoring yourself in this way. You don't need to fight or silence it; just be aware it is not your highest self talking. Each person is a unique expression of energy. With pink, you take the time to love all of yourself and recognize the perfection in your individual "snowflakiness."

THE SHADOW SIDE OF PINK

The shadow side of pink is self-criticism and can also manifest as being judgmental of others. There are many physical signs someone is struggling with pink energy, including depression, eating disorders, or addiction to plastic surgery. If you lean toward the shadow side of pink, you will resist acknowledging your own strength, beauty, and power. Some of these exercises may trigger you, and your mind will think you are not being authentic, that you are ignoring your "flaws." Resistance is common when you are trying to access self-love. The mistake many people make is trying to disagree with this negativity. The secret is in knowing that it only thrives when you engage with it.

It is important to remember a core truth of your being is a deep sense of calm, peace, and serenity. Self-love doesn't mean you are devoid of any negative thought. Rather, pink will help train your dominant voice to be more loving and positive. If you are leaning toward the shadow side of pink, be patient. Pink will first highlight some of your critical thinking if there is an abundance of it, and then, with calm awareness, replace those thoughts with something more positive.

If you do notice negative thoughts popping up as you activate pink, don't fight them or criticize yourself for having them. Simply keep reminding yourself that you are exactly who you are supposed to be, where you are supposed to be, and that you are doing a perfect job on your journey. Allow the loving, nurturing energy of pink to wash over you.

This week, try to focus on "patting yourself on the back." Pink light reminds to us to step back and observe how far we have come. Give yourself permission to be happy with who you are.

CHAPTER 11

❖

MINT GREEN

QUALITIES: Enthusiasm, change, and life force
SHADOW SIDE: Hyperactivity, anxiety, and poor health

Mint green is associated with growth of all kinds. Just like the plant itself, mint easily grabs hold of the earth and springs to life. I find this to be quite symbolic of the way I see lighter green energy, as our physical bodies are constantly regenerating themselves. Since it is the color of new plants and leaves, lighter green is usually the color most associated with the new life that occurs in nature. The green color of plants is primarily caused by chlorophyll, the chemical that allows plants to convert sunlight into usable energy. Quite literally, green helps all living things to thrive and grow into what the universe intended them to be.

In many languages, even the word *green* has the same root as the word *grow*, further solidifying their association. Germanic, Romance, Slavic, and Hellenic languages all contain words for green that originate from words for vibrant, living plants. The Japanese word for green is *midori*, which evolved from the word *midoru*, meaning "to blossom" or "to grow."

Historically, light green is associated with new life and growth. In ancient Rome, green was the color of Venus, the goddess of gardens and vegetables. Ancient Egyptians associated green with the new crops that sprouted as a result of the annual flooding of the Nile River. In addition, Egyptian hieroglyphs for green portray a growing papyrus sprout, while wall paintings of the god Osiris show him with a green face, which was the symbol of good health and rebirth. In China, green has long been considered an auspicious color that symbolizes fertility and happiness.

"Electric mint green" may sound like a unique way to describe a color, but it is the closest I can come to explaining how I see this energy around people. Not only that, but mint green is one of the only colors I can almost *hear*. It is so filled with new life that it has a kind of hum to it. Whenever I teach classes on color energy, I always end with mint as the final color. Mint green represents change and new opportunities, which is why I save this color for last. This is exactly the kind of energy I want to leave you with.

This journey through color that we have embarked upon has allowed us to explore and bring out so many elements of the soul. With this in mind, it seems fitting to now recognize the changes possible in our lives with this particular color.

Mint green represents our life force, often referred to as chi or prana. I see this color as the life energy radiating from our soul. Mint green is a direct reflection of our health and well-being, but that is not all. It crosses the border of physical wellness and also reflects on how we approach our personal growth on the planet. Enthusiasm is such a huge element of mint green. When this color is dominant in someone's energy field, they are the most effective cheerleader anyone could hope for and are excellent at manifesting. Mint green energy is welcome in every situation because it makes everyone feel like anything is possible. If you've ever turned a day of household chores into an impromptu dance party, you've generated a shot of this fun-loving energy. I often joke that if you tell a mint green person you are having a garage sale, they will be the first to show up at your house with coffee, signs, music, and snacks.

In my private practice, I often see mint around pregnant women. Mint green energy is filled with so much life that it radiates from mothers-to-be as they are creating new life for the planet. Mint green feels like "cosmic caffeine." It radiates so quickly I can almost hear it. The tone isn't distracting in any way, but just like birds chirping or waves crashing, it's a subtle and beautiful reminder that we are alive.

Kenneth was a client of mine whom I had been coaching for years. Naturally energetic and highly creative, he was a hairstylist who was always *doing* something. Kenneth had overcome a serious drug addiction and, like many people in recovery, now channeled much of his energy into work. I had coached him into opening his own hair salon in NYC, and he had created a very successful life for himself.

For most clients, the colors I see around them change with time due to life circumstances. But this was never the case with Kenneth. He was constantly buzzing with the same mint green, almost like a hummingbird.

"Dougall, I just can't seem to calm down," Kenneth lamented.

"What do you mean?"

"Things are great; business is booming. I am generally happy, but it's hard for me to relax, and I have a tendency to worry about everything."

"I understand. Sometimes it can be difficult to turn the volume down on our lives. Are you meditating?"

"Ha! Are you kidding? Anytime I try to meditate, my fingers are tapping, my feet are moving."

This is another interesting aspect of mint green. It is a powerhouse of energy, but sometimes it can be *too much* energy if left unchecked. You may remember, back in high school, looking at other students sitting at their desks with their feet tapping on the floor repeatedly. They couldn't sit still or concentrate for very long and seemed like they were going to burst out of their chairs. This is what too much mint green feels like.

You may have had similar experiences with people like this, or perhaps you are the one who had an overabundance of energy. Mint green is great as long as you know how (and when) to turn it off. Kenneth's mint green energy was overflowing and the "off" button seemed to be just out of his reach.

As with every color, there are two sides to its energy. For someone like me, finding my center in meditation is quite easy. On the other hand, I can lean toward being a bit lazy if I am not careful. A dose of mint green energizes me to partake in physical activity. I often activate this color before I head to the gym for the boost it provides. For someone like Kenneth, who has a ton of mint energy, sitting still and meditating is almost torture. His energy can lean into the shadow side of mint green, which he described as hyperactivity and some anxiety. These kinds of energy types usually have a very high metabolism. (As someone who has lost over 90 pounds in my lifetime, that sounds like a wonderful problem to have!)

"Kenneth, you always radiate this electric mint green from your aura. Having a ton of energy is a great thing, and you have been using it to create the life you want. It has allowed you to build a thriving business you are passionate about, which most people would love. However, staying in this energy constantly is not sustainable, and it sounds like you are dealing with an imbalance of mint green energy.

Your body knows this, which is why you are beginning to feel burned out. We need to bring balance to your being. Because your physical body is such a dominant part of your energy, we need to find a routine that will help you slow down your energy and find your center."

"I don't see how that is possible. I feel like my mind always keeps me from relaxing, even when I try to sit still and meditate."

I hear this from people all the time—these judgments that we self-impose on our lives as to how our spirituality is supposed to look. There are so many roads to peace and enlightenment. I believe each soul on the planet has a unique perspective on how to find their personal balance and their best center. I can learn a lot from a mint green energy like Kenneth's. Dynamic movement, life force, and energy all come very naturally to him. A mint green person bounces out of bed, as they are a classic morning person. My energy type is naturally closer to an aura color that resembles a vanilla latte—preferably served on a comfy sofa while I relax for two hours and meditate on the events of the day. Then I would eventually motivate myself to generate that kind of energy.

"When do you feel it is most challenging for you to find your center?" I asked Kenneth.

"It's usually at the end of the day. I recognize that I have been productive, that I have had a full day, and yet I still can't quiet my mind. I always have this feeling I may have forgotten something, or that I could do more. Some of my friends say I seem jittery."

I realized that, in Kenneth's case, sitting still and spiritually activating mint green would only cause more distraction for him. Instead, I offered him a way to harness his natural energy and channel it into a healthy relationship with mint green.

"Kenneth, let's try honoring your natural rhythm. I would like to test out merging exercise with your meditation. I want you to select a workout but set an intention that you will visualize mint green energy pouring down through your body as you do it. Try to pick something that will help you release your energy but that will also allow you to quiet your mind. When you do this, try to stay away from any sport or exercise requiring you to talk with other people. Interaction is normally great, but we want to use this time as a quiet meditation for you. Jogging, yoga, or taking a spin class would all be great examples of exercise that would blend well with your spiritual activation. Right before you begin, take some deep breaths and see mint green light above your head. Then imagine it pouring down through your body as you continue to exercise."

My intention here was for Kenneth to honor his natural chemistry in an effort to help balance it out. In his case, there was so much energy coursing through his being that we needed to find a way to release it. On a spiritual level, it felt like he was left with an abundance of concentrated energy after overcoming addiction, and he understandably needed to direct it elsewhere. Kenneth was feeling judgmental of himself for not being able to meditate in a traditional way, and I wanted to help free him of those self-made requirements. By first releasing the expectation of how to find peace and aligning with his natural energy, I felt this would be the best way for him to access his center.

A week later, Kenneth and I had a follow-up session. He sat down and was excited to talk about the outcome.

"Wow, Dougall, this was an interesting experience."

"Tell me everything!"

"I decided to go for a run every day for 45 minutes. Exercise is not a new thing for me, but normally it's a very social thing I do with friends. I regularly go to the gym and either run on the treadmill or take a class, but always with friends. This time, instead of listening to music or running with a friend, I did what you said and set the intention that this exercise was my meditation. I went to the park and pictured mint green as I ran around the reservoir. At the end of every run, I did notice I felt more calm and relaxed. Even though it wasn't the way I would normally picture meditation, I did feel like it was helping me quiet my mind. At the end of the week, I also had some interesting awareness of how much I had been judging myself."

"What do you mean?"

"When I was a child, my family would make fun of my inability to sit still. They liked to call me 'Crazy Kenneth.' On long car rides, I would tap the window of the car. It wasn't even a conscious thing. The tapping gave me something to do until it annoyed someone. I would always pace during family gatherings. Even in school, I would get in trouble for moving too much. Nobody knew anything about ADHD [attention deficit hyperactivity disorder] in those days, and they just assumed I didn't like school. I don't think I ever fully came to grips with how much shame I had around my energy. This experiment really shifted my thought about it. Rather than judge my energy level and see it as a bad thing, I was able, with the help of mint green, to move it into a positive place in my mind, to see it as just another expression of my soul."

I love the way mint green energy can bring about new perspectives. In that moment, it gives us a change of thought, the ability to see our issue from a different perspective. Electric mint green is about joy, fun, and our natural state of mind.

I am not a fan of strenuous physical exercise. However, I know it is important for my health, so I do it. When I reflect upon it, I think my resistance to exercise may have to do with being a sexual abuse survivor. Whereas meditation helps me leave my physical body, exercise forces me to be completely present in my body, and that can sometimes be uncomfortable. Nonetheless, I work with mint green to help ground an awareness of my own energy.

For my personal approach to mint green, I don't use exercise as a physical meditation to quiet my mind. The challenge for me is to be fully awake and present in my body as I work out. I can quiet my mind so easily with meditation, but what about using mint green to fully engage and awaken my energy?

When I activate mint green before exercise, it really allows me to feel and stay present in my body. It guides me in the awareness of how my energy is flowing. As I stay in a stretch longer to become more flexible, or lift one more rep so I can be stronger, and even as I pay attention to how my body responds to certain foods, mint has helped me stay physically present in my body. In a nutshell, mint green has helped me directly connect with my life force and wellness. It is still an ongoing process, but I enjoy learning about myself. And I often find my best ideas come to me during some kind of physical exercise.

ACTIVATING MINT GREEN NOTES

AM I FULLY ALIVE AND PRESENT IN MY BODY?

I like to think of activating mint green as a graduation of sorts. This is not because you are ending the process, but because this represents your graduation into a new and powerful journey through the possibilities of color. Mint green is a symbol of your awakened relationship with color, and it symbolizes the various positive adjustments you can implement with every color. I typically see mint green around kids who are giggling and people who are in great physical health. It creates a zest for life and is a very physically tangible color.

When you activate this energy, it is almost impossible for your mind to comprehend how quickly it moves. With silver, I encouraged you to take your time to experience the depth and nuanced pace of that energy. As you start working with electric mint green, the experience will be almost the opposite of that. Let mint green move through your physical body as quickly as it wants to. If it makes you want to dance, then turn on your favorite music and go for it. If it makes you want to hike in nature or take on a new home-improvement project, then do so. Allow this energy to activate your body and create new possibilities for growth, because that physical activity will translate to new beginnings in other areas as well. Most people report feeling joy, excitement, and a sense of positive motivation for the future.

SPIRITUAL ACTIVATION NOTES

Many of us make our meditation and spiritual practice a private, tranquil affair. We light candles and have soft music playing in the privacy of our homes, using the moment to leave our bodies and experience another realm of consciousness. These are great ways to connect with the sanctity of our inner being, and I highly recommend doing private meditation on a regular basis. But mint green energy wants to be seen in order to flourish, the same way plants need to be "seen" by the sun in order to grow. Mint green energy is more about an active meditation, a physical experience rather than self-reflection.

I do recommend a traditional seated visualization with mint green before a romantic date. This color helps to open your energy and will activate the part of you that wants to ask questions and meet new people. It will also help to keep the mood light, which is useful when you first get to know another person. Being authentically you is important in the long run, but delving too emotionally deep at first is often a misguided attempt to rush intimacy. Wearing mint is not the only way to activate this energy, as you can still invoke this positive and upbeat energy with a spiritual activation.

SPIRITUAL ACTIVATION EXERCISE: TAKE IT OUTSIDE!

Because of mint green's optimistic and energetic nature, your spiritual activation with green will be slightly different from the others. You will be doing the visualization in conjunction with some kind of physical activity. When spiritually activating mint green, being in nature is a wonderful way to further release its positive energy.

1. Think of a way to merge your spiritual activation with a physical activity. Since you will be spiritually activating mint green as you do this exercise, your eyes will mostly be open. The main element of this activation is to see the energy ground down through your body and then pour deep into the core of the earth. There are many ways you can do this exercise. Gardening can be a great way to envision mint green energy directly beneath your feet as you are standing on the dirt. Cooking is a wonderful way to activate green as you create a nourishing meal. One of my favorite ways to activate mint green is by playing music as I cook, which

usually includes me singing into a spatula "microphone." Just about any physical exercise is a great match for spiritually activating mint green, from yoga to spin class and beyond.

2. Try to incorporate multiple senses as you carry this activation out, and continue to ground mint energy through your body. Mint green usually incorporates more than one sense as it awakens and exhilarates the spirit. If you are on a beach walk as you activate green, let the waves naturally speak to you. *Listen* to the sound of the surf, *look* at the waves as they swell, *feel* the soft sand beneath your feet, and *smell* the salty air of the ocean. Every incoming wave crashing onto the shore symbolizes a burst of positive energy, while every time the water retreats back to the ocean represents anything that is no longer serving.

3. This idea of focusing multiple senses on your activation can be used no matter what activity you choose to do. A simple hike or even a stroll through your neighborhood can turn into a conscious mint green meditation, with crunching leaves beneath your feet, the brisk breeze on your face, and the smell of pine needles in the air. The ultimate goal is to utilize as many senses as possible to assist you in this activation. These added elements will help keep you grounded and present in your body while connecting with divine mint green energy. I am a big believer in conscious meditation, and this exercise will demonstrate how any activity can become a rejuvenating ritual.

UNIVERSAL ACTIVATION NOTES
(AKA "I SPY" WITH MY INTUITIVE EYE)

When you activate mint green, it will highlight your enthusiasm for life. I once took a series of Pilates classes for the first time, which triggered some strong emotions for me. Pilates is very slow, there is no music, and we had to be very mindful and present with our bodies. Nonetheless, I had picked this new form of exercise as my commitment to mint green energy. There was one particular movement where we lowered ourselves to the ground with one leg crossed over the other, arriving in a sort of cross-legged seat on the floor. After we achieved that position and sat for a few moments with some deep breathing, the teacher instructed us to stand up. The goal was to get off the ground on your own, without using your hands. She explained: "Studies have shown that there is a direct correlation in both longevity and quality of life among people who can get up off the floor by themselves."

Basically, if you could get up off the ground without using your hands, it was a good sign of how independent you will be later in life. It was such a simple movement, but it brought up a lot of feelings for me because I could not fully do it. I think I needed to place a couple of my fingertips on the floor for balance, and the flood of emotions affected me. Feeling frustrated after a few weeks of this, I looked across the room and noticed one of the other students was sitting on a mint green yoga mat. *Okay,* I thought to myself. I acknowledged this as a universal activation from the universe and vowed to continue practicing.

This exercise class included such a seemingly simple movement, and yet it was a deep reflection of my genetic history. In my family, several of my loved ones cannot get themselves up off the floor due to mobility issues. I know this to be true, as I have witnessed it firsthand at family gatherings. I have seen loved ones struggle with physical mobility in everyday-life kinds of ways. And although this color is used for all kinds of new beginnings, energetic mint green has helped me realize I will always make physical activity a priority in my life.

I may joke about struggling to muster up energy in the morning. And sure, a glass of chardonnay on a breezy terrace is way more appealing to me than a Pilates class. However, the more and more that I ground mint green energy into my physical routine, the more I understand and appreciate its purpose. Not only do I want to be able to pop up from the ground well into my nineties, but I want to love and honor my body so I am available for many years of new beginnings.

UNIVERSAL ACTIVATION EXERCISE: TRY SOMETHING NEW

Mint green energy is useful to help you step out of your comfort zone and see what new experiences you can manifest. Your journey with color can represent a new endeavor in your life, and new beginnings are perfectly encapsulated in this color. Electric mint green shakes things up, which is necessary for positive growth. Dr. Joe Dispenza has written many books showing the neuroscientific correlation between changing our routine and living a happier, more fulfilling life. Many studies have shown that when we stay in any kind of routine for too long, our brains and bodies move into autopilot. This is also true with life experiences. There is an absolute beauty to the comfort and familiarity of routine. But in order to fully align with the law of attraction, we must be open to accessing new and different parts of our consciousness.

Whenever you spot mint green and have a universal activation, allow it to be a sign for you to try something new that day. This can be an intention that you set, or it can be spontaneous if you just happen to notice the color some-where. Whenever you see it, think of some kind of new activity you can try. It does not have to be anything major, as long as it is new for you. It can be as simple as ordering something new for lunch, starting a conversation with someone you don't know, or going to a different supermarket for your grocery shopping. The intention with this exercise is to harness mint green to help you activate and attract new possibilities. Other activities could include going to a new museum or exploring a nearby town you have never been to.

As you try this new activity or undertaking, check in with yourself regularly to see how it is affecting the energy of your physical body. Feel free to keep notes on this in your journal if you like. You may feel a variety of things, but look for the overall reaction. It may feel unfamiliar, but if you're having fun and expanding your consciousness, you are on to something good that you should repeat!

Every time you see vibrant light green, think of it as your dose of cosmic caffeine. Affirm with each sighting you are open to change and fully connected to the law of attraction. This electric mint green makes you feel excitement and joy for your life. It also teaches you to be grateful to be alive and in your body.

MINT GREEN AFFIRMATION

I AM FULLY PRESENT IN MY BODY.

PHYSICAL ACTIVATION NOTES

Physical activation with mint green can be a helpful tool in manifesting. One aspect of my career I particularly love is that

I regularly get to travel to Japan. Each time I go, I host a series of lectures, workshops, and a variety of private readings and coaching sessions. This has been the most amazing experience, and I am profoundly grateful for the opportunity to connect with clients there. I have always felt a connection to a past life in Japan, and being there truly feels like being home.

Physically activating mint green helped open my consciousness to the possibility of wonderful, fulfilling connections in Japan. As an exercise in manifesting and to send out a clear message of intention to the universe, I decided to take Japanese language classes when I was first put in contact with my Japanese colleagues. I kept my notes in a mint green notebook and would touch it to remind myself of my intention to speak Japanese *in* Japan. Most days it felt like a great idea, but there were others when I felt completely frustrated by it. Did you know the Japanese language has *three* separate alphabets, one of which is completely composed of symbols? It has been quite a challenge, but I am determined to learn how to converse in Japanese.

When I am in Japanese class, I can feel parts of my brain firing off electrons that have been dormant for quite some time. Memorization, pronunciation, writing, and reading a completely new alphabet have grounded me into my body in a way I never expected. It is both exciting and terrifying at the same time. If I ever feel self-critical of my level of comprehension, I just touch my notebook and remind myself of my intention behind these classes. Although it was difficult to start, I am proud to say I now have a *very* basic knowledge of conversational Japanese. This is helpful because I just returned from my third trip to Japan and have another one planned!

My next goal is to lead a meditation in Japanese. And although I don't know how long it may take me to master the vocabulary, I will use mint green to help me manifest this dream!

Some mint green color props you could incorporate into your day include:

- **Fresh mint.** Get a potted mint plant to keep in your home. Not only is this a great color prop, but the leaves can also be incorporated into your meals.

- **A mint green scarf.** Mint green is a lovely color to wear, and placing it around your neck ensures you can see and touch it throughout your day.

- **Matcha green tea.** Packed with antioxidants and vitamin C, matcha (along with gunpowder tea, another form of green tea) is a wonderful way to enjoy mint green energy. Add some almond milk to transform it into a perfectly hued latte!

PHYSICAL ACTIVATION EXERCISE: MANIFEST WITH MINT

Set an intention for something you would like to manifest in your life. (Note: This exercise will complement just about any other manifesting process you are using.)

Make sure to write your intention down somewhere you can easily see it. This can be a vision board, your desktop background, a message taped onto your bathroom mirror, or anything else like this. For ideas, think of a hobby, class, cuisine, trip, or experience you have always wanted to try. What could you incorporate into your life that would be new, different, and uplifting? We live in a magical time when knowledge and experience are right at our fingertips. When we are open to something new, we expand our energy and create passion in our lives.

Select a mint green color prop to use for physically activating this energy. You can change the item as often as you like. Touch this item whenever you want a reminder of your goal.

Much like orange, mint green is easy to incorporate through food, because you can go out and buy fresh mint to keep around the house. Not only do you physically activate it through touch, but it also smells amazing, which brings another sense in to your color prop. I'm not sure I have ever met anyone who doesn't appreciate the smell or taste of fresh mint. Add it to water or food, or just use it as a bouquet in your home and notice its fresh, uplifting effect on your mood.

The world of nature is an excellent color prop, and I recommend bringing it into your home as often as possible Every shade of green is represented in nature, so find a vibrant green plant and use it as an intentional reminder for new possibilities in your life.

If you are looking for a little bit of extra attention, mint green is a great color to incorporate into your wardrobe. It can easily make you the most magnetic person in the room.

THE SHADOW SIDE OF MINT GREEN

The shadow side of mint green is anxiety and struggles with physical health. Anxiety is often the fear of unknown outcomes, which is why it directly counteracts the energy of mint green. If you find you are resisting the color and leaning toward the shadow side, there is a chance you may have trouble being fully present in your body. You may know someone who is like a tornado of energy. As soon as they walk into the room, papers are immediately flying everywhere as they try to find their keys and talk about four different topics at once. They are great people, but it just feels like they need to slow down for a second and catch their breath.

This kind of whirlwind energy is a sign of a mint green imbalance. Because mint green helps us to feel our body, it has a strong, almost viscerally kinetic response. For some people, an imbalance of this energy can feel like anxiety. If such is the case for you, a slower form of exercise can be a helpful addition to balance this energy. Tai Chi, yoga, creating pottery, or a quiet walk around the block are good ways to utilize mint green in a way that should feel safer. It can take some time to get comfortable combining your spiritual practice with physical activity.

AFTERWORD

❖

FOLLOW YOUR RAINBOW

People often ask me to describe what an aura, or the energy around someone, looks like. It is almost impossible for me to express the depth and magnitude of our energy structures. And, in reality, it would be naive of me to think I am seeing the full picture of our energetic bodies. I can only convey what *I* see around people as I continue working in my chosen field. It reminds me of stargazing. You can lie down on the grass and stare up at our universe for hours. Your eyes will focus on perhaps one twinkling light. You may even notice a constellation and think you have a grasp on what is really up there. But the truth is, we all experience the depth and tremendous scope of the universe in our own way.

It is the same for our soul and the energies we radiate. I may see one, two, or even three colors around someone when I give a reading, but our souls are so profound and our experiences, as well as our energies, are constantly changing. I may see one color around a client, and then, a year later, I will see a completely different color, depending on what is going on in their life. That is why I wanted to familiarize you with the ten major colors individually. Just as your life will continue to change, the colors and energy you reach for will continue to change.

I have described these colors based on my own interpretations of many clients' personality traits. But this is filtered through my own lens of understanding the universe. Categorizing color energy is almost like asking a shooting star to pause so we can examine and try to understand it. However, I feel that the energies these colors represent are universal. I have created a system that will help you explore some of the more dominant aspects of your life. From activating higher thought forms with gold to discovering your destiny and purpose with purple, these colors will help you adjust and strengthen the qualities of yourself as you need them.

The changes you have the power to make are endless, from focusing on the state of your home with silver to optimizing your relationship with your physical body through mint green. This system provides you the opportunity to reflect and take stock of where you are and, most importantly, where you want to go. Utilizing this process helps you build a sense of balance using colors you have been seeing all your life. This is an opportunity to take the reins on key life components using a variety of senses.

There are so many ways to naturally bring color and light energy into your life. It is completely up to you how much you want to utilize the power of these colors. You could work your way through every color, week by week until you have made a complete circle of color energy. You can repeat the process from start to finish, starting with white. Or you can refer back to each color as needed, calling upon specific colors to guide you when you need them most. My main goal is to show you that color is a new language you can use.

I go through phases of energy and will intermittently be drawn to different colors, depending on where I am in life. For example, I am currently in a blue phase. I noticed the other day while clothing shopping that I had picked a pair of blue shorts, a blue polo, several blue T-shirts, and blue socks. I even recently bought new blue pillows for our living room. But instead of just shrugging and saying "I like blue," I pay attention to see what my energy is telling me through that color.

In moments like these, it may not be immediately apparent what the color is trying to tell you. For me, I knew that blue energy was trying to tell me something about my life. So let's explore this together. I have mentioned that often with blue, the clairvoyant imagery for me is stacks and stacks of blue books. When I had my little blue shopping spree, I was just in the final leg of finishing this book. If I am being honest with myself and am tuning in to the message behind blue, I must admit that I had quite a bit of fear during the writing process. The combination of expressing my ideas, concepts, and processes seems to bring up some fear of rejection and failure. Being creative means making myself vulnerable.

As these fears began popping up, I naturally started to surround myself with blue. But I also noticed the color blue was popping out at me regularly during my day. Focusing on its meaning pointed out I had some subconscious fear floating around my energy. Once you have made a relationship with each color and have grounded it through your being, it can become your own divination system. The universe will use color as a way to communicate and connect with you. It may seem hard to decipher at first, kind of like my attempts at learning Japanese. But once you take the time to get familiar with it, you will find yourself recognizing and receiving information through color.

That's just the beginning. So often we wait for the universe to speak to us through signs. Many people say they
would like a sign from the universe. By living your life in color,
you empower yourself to create energy and change in your
life with the use of color. Now that you have a strong sense of
and connection to the ten most practical colors for our lives,
you can use them in any order or way you see fit. Depending on your circumstances, you can activate any color from
an emotional, spiritual, or physical (or, preferably, all of the
above) perspective. This process can help you be your best
self and keep your energy managed, as it did for me recently.

I was invited to do a live speaking event at the Oprah
Winfrey Network in Los Angeles. They have a program for
their employees called OWN University, or OWN U. Some of
the OWN U speakers have included Brené Brown, Iyanla Van-
zant, Cameron Diaz, and, on this particular day, me. Gulp. I
had spent a few weeks with this on my calendar and I was
trying to pretend that it wasn't that big of a deal. There had
already been several conference call meetings with the people at OWN. We also talked about recording some videos for
Oprah.com before my live presentation for around 70 execu-
tives and team members.

"Um, will Oprah be there?" I asked during one of the
conference calls.

"She might be. It depends on whether or not she is in the
building."

I have lived in LA for over eight years now. Some of my
clients are quite well known, and at this point I have gotten
used to meeting celebrities. Once you see that everyone deals
with the same fundamental problems and challenges, the
illusion really fades. Having said that, there are a few people
that the thought of meeting makes me a little nervous, and
one of them is Oprah Winfrey. The grounded, rational part

of my being knows that she is human just like everyone else. However, the kid in me that would cut school and watch her show religiously had a hard time understanding the idea of sharing air space with her.

It would be one thing to meet her at an event or a party. I would probably introduce myself nervously and ask if she wanted to talk about spirituality over blueberry scones sometime. But the idea I could be standing at the front of a room she was in, giving a spiritually uplifting talk based on my work, was giving me all the feels. Exciting as this was, I could feel myself turning into a nervous wreck.

Usually I can compartmentalize parts of my personality. I can use purple on days I need to step into being a leader. I will invoke emerald green when I need to write or express myself. Using electric mint green helps me bring vitality and a youthful joy to things. Each color helps me have laser focus on an energy or part of my consciousness. But this felt like a lot to manage. This would be the combination of being in my power as a teacher and potentially meeting a hugely inspiring teacher of mine.

The morning of the talk, I was unsure what color to wear. I decided to use my shower as my meditation space. I like combining my shower and meditation. It's cleansing, and there are no distractions. There is also something poetic about washing my physical body while also creating quiet space and "washing" my spiritual self.

On this particular morning, during my shower meditation, my mind was racing. There was very little quiet, peaceful energy. What I realized was there were two very powerful energies dancing through my mind. The spiritual teacher inside me wanted to do well and be invited back. The young student inside me just wanted to play it cool if Oprah decided to make a cameo appearance.

"I need to be grounded," I said out loud.

I quickly decided it was imperative for me to wear black. You see, black represents grounding energy. The earth, soil, and all matter are invoked through black energy. It is the color that grounds our being to the planet. People often ask me about color energy, and then they will say: "What about black? Do you ever see black in someone's aura?" Or they will joke in reference to a negative person, "I bet that person's aura is black." This sort of remark is often stated as if black energy is a bad thing. But this is a misconception. Why would one color be inherently negative? They all have a positive side and a shadow side. Visually, black is said to absorb all other colors, which to me is a perfect example of its grounding power. Black has the capability to take all of our scattered energy and root us into the core of the earth.

When I lived in New York City, black was my signature color for clothing. In fact, many people in Manhattan enjoy wearing black. This is not just because it is slimming. I think it's because physical space is extremely limited in big cities. I would go from a crowded street down to a packed subway car, to finally arrive at my tiny office. At the end of the day, I would reverse this trek to then return to my small apartment. So, to protect our energy, we pull it inward. Someone from a smaller town might think New Yorkers aren't friendly, and I understand why. We tend to be very focused on where we are going, and we usually avoid eye contact on trains. But when we feel scattered or overwhelmed, it is natural to want to pull our energy close to ourselves. Very dark brown, black, charcoal gray, and other dark, earthy tones are useful for grounding us and protecting our own energy.

Now that I am living in Los Angeles, my wardrobe has shifted to brighter colors as I have more space. But, on this particular day, black seemed to be calling strongly to me.

When we use black as our color, it is the one time we reverse the activation process. As I was dressing for my event at OWN, rather than envisioning black six inches above my head, I envisioned two spheres of black energy just below my feet. These black spheres of energy take on an interesting visual for me. If you have ever seen the stone obsidian, that is very similar to what I see. There are golden hues mixed into the black stone. You could even describe it as iridescent.

For every color except black, during the activation process we are looking to the heavens and the universe for our guidance. We are reminding ourselves of our soul body. But when we work with earth tones, we are doing the exact opposite. The reason we focus below our feet with earth tones like black is to help ground our energy into the planet. On this day, I needed to express spiritual topics in a grounded way that was palatable for everyone.

We are all multifaceted beings, and we wear several hats during our day. You may be a mom, wife, lawyer, friend, Reiki practitioner, and avid Duran Duran groupie all at once. Depending on the task at hand, you lead with whatever part of your identity is called upon. There are a few key moments in life when we get to wear all hats at once. And on that day at the Oprah Winfrey Network, I wanted to wear them all. I was so nervous, so out of my body, but I needed to be present. I wanted to be connected and fully integrated into this experience. I also wanted to be balanced and in a unified place.

I put on a black V-neck sweater as my last moment of conscious meditation. I affirmed to myself that every time I saw the color black that day, I would harness my energy and give it a dose of grounded centeredness.

When David and I arrived at the OWN studios, we climbed the steps to the lobby, and David immediately started laughing.

"Oh my gosh, how fun!"

"What?"

We opened the door, and right in front of us was a giant, floor-to-ceiling video screen with my image on it and a message that said: *The Oprah Winfrey Network Welcomes Dougall Fraser.*

Now, in theory, this type of moment should have caused me to get all kinds of freaked out. I was already feeling nervous to be speaking there, and now everyone who walked by could see my face. It would have been very easy for me not to give myself permission to have fun with this moment. I was busy wearing my spiritual teacher hat, and somehow I assumed a spiritual teacher wouldn't get excited about that sort of thing.

But today was different. Today, I was grounded. I had activated black to help me be all things in the present moment, and in this moment I was so flattered. All I could do was giggle. We walked up to the front desk, where I pointed to the wall and said, "Hi, that's me on the wall over there." David begged me to stand in front of it for a photo. We sat down on the plush benches, waiting for the OWN team and staring at my picture in front of us.

When the OWN team came down, we were escorted up to a room where we would shoot the videos. I was introduced to Samantha, who would be interviewing me for the segments, and as I shook her hand, I was drawn to a necklace that she was wearing. It was the most beautiful amulet, a black obsidian stone wrapped in golden wire. It was right in front of me, and it was a perfect manifestation of universal activation. I explained to her the process of why I activated black and how her necklace was helping me calm my nerves.

We proceeded to film a series of short videos, and, if I do say so myself, I nailed it. The grounding energy of black (and my ability to spy it in real time) helped me make a smooth transition from being excited in the lobby into clearly delivering wisdom and information without skipping a beat.

My talk for OWN U was scheduled to be taped at 5 P.M. in front of an audience of about 60 people. I had some extra time before the talk, so David and I went to the on-site café to get a snack and some refreshments. The café is designed to look like a lovely lounge, with beautifully upholstered furniture at one end and a gorgeous kitchen filled with goodies at the other end. I helped myself to a coffee and a snack, then sat down quietly. Almost immediately, my mind filled with chatter: *This coffee is delicious, and so is this gluten-free cookie. Wait a minute, are these some of Oprah's favorite things? I mean, this is her office, so there's a good chance that those are Julia Roberts's favorite muffins over there.*

Finally it was time to begin the talk, and I felt like my body had been plugged into an electric socket. A combination of energy, excitement, and nerves was coursing through me. As I was talking, I could feel my breath getting ahead of me. It was like cosmic caffeine multiplied by 100. In that moment, I started to judge myself. Critical thoughts circled through my mind: *A spiritual teacher would be calm. A real teacher would speak slowly. What kind of spiritual teacher starts to sweat during their presentation?*

In that moment, while talking, I decided I needed a little break. I would walk the walk and do a brief, conscious meditation. A voice in my head said, *Just breathe. You are allowed to pause and regroup.* So, without a thought, I told the group that I needed a moment to stop and breathe. I took a sip of water, closed my eyes, and took a few deep breaths. I looked down at my black sweater and reminded myself of my intention.

I turned to the side. Some of the OWN staff sweetly applauded and cheered for a moment. I took a deep breath, and I went back to owning my power. (Get it, OWNing?)

We all experience self-doubt at some point in our lives. Black helped me optimize my energy, but I was still feeling exhilaration and some nervousness. It retrospect, it's funny to me I struggled with giving myself permission to reconnect. Rather than pretending this day wasn't a big deal or I wasn't excited, I wanted to experience this moment as fully as possible. Part of my consciousness was focused on my inner child, that overweight gay kid who used to watch the Oprah show every day, looking for inspiration. Let me tell you, he was jumping for joy that day, and I made sure to honor him by acknowledging the excitement.

But another part of my consciousness was the teacher who had been doing spiritual work for over 18 years, fully intending to teach and uplift this group of people. It made perfect sense to me I would need a moment to regroup and breathe. By grounding myself, I made sure I was as present in that moment as I could be. The rest of the talk went quite well, and I am proud of myself for being both human and teacher in the same breath. After my talk, I stayed to speak with some of the audience members. Then David and I hopped into our car to race over to our Japanese language class. In a full day, I was able to be a fan, an enthusiastic human, a nervous person, a teacher, a student, and an intuitive. Throughout all this, I was constantly using the power of color as my guide.

The layout of this day is the perfect example of how color can play a role in our lives. I have harnessed these energies effectively for many years, and I hope they will work just as well for you and that you feel you have the tools to incorporate energy on every level. What I have come to know is we must approach our lives with a certain level of balance. When we merge the worlds of spirit, body, and emotion, we elevate our energy to its purest form.

There are times when we can get stuck in one dimension or another. On the day that I described, I started with my meditation and set my intention to be grounded and fully integrated. I activated the color on a spiritual level with my visualization. I then activated the color on a physical level, with the color prop being my black sweater. I affirmed the universe would guide me with mini messages by helping me spy the color during my day to remind me of my intention. The result was a fully integrated, powerfully rewarding experience.

If I could leave you with one main suggestion in regards to color energy, it would be this: don't worry too much about choosing the "right" color to activate in your life. Now that you have this guide and more awareness of color, you know that color has more power to it than just being something pretty for our eyes. Rather than trying to think of the perfect color for you, you can just start using them. Each one will create exciting changes in your energy, and you can continue to adjust how much you use each one. Take note of how they affect you, and if you experience any color differently than I do, great! The important thing is to just dive in and *use* them.

Thank you so much for taking the time to explore the powerful world of color with me. I have done this work for close to 20 years and absolutely love introducing its potential to people. You now have many tools to help you go forward with color in unlimited ways. Give it a try, and please let me know how it works for you!

ENDNOTES

❖

Chapter 6

1. Donald A. Laird, "Fatigue: Public Enemy Number One; What It Is and How to Fight It," *American Journal of Nursing* 33, no. 9 (September 1933): 835–841.

2. "A Flash of Green Enhances Creativity," *Pacific Standard,* March 20, 2012, http://www.psmag.com/books-and-culture/a-flash-of-green-enhances-creativity-40483. See also Stephanie Lichtenfeld et al., "Fertile Green: Green Facilitates Creative Performance," *Personality and Social Psychology Bulletin* 38, no. 6 (June 2012): 784–797.

3. See, for instance, Sylvie Studentea, Nina Seppalab, and Noemi Sadowskaa, "Facilitating Creative Thinking in the Classroom: Investigating the Effects of Plants and the Colour Green on Visual and Verbal Creativity," *Thinking Skills and Creativity* 19 (March 2016): 1–8. http://www.sciencedirect.com/science/article/pii/ S1871187115300250.

4. Gretchen Reynolds, "Greenery (or Even Photos of Trees) Can Make Us Happier," *Well* (blog), *The New York Times,* March 17, 2016, http:// well.blogs.nytimes.com/2016/03/17/the-picture-of-health.

Chapter 8

5. "Psychological Study Reveals That Red Enhances Men's Attraction to Women," PhysOrg.Com, October 28, 2008. Available online at http:// medicalxpress.com/news/2008-10-psychological-reveals-red-men-women.html.

Chapter 10

6. A. G. Schauss, "Application of Behavioral Photobiology to Human Aggression: Baker-Miller Pink," *International Journal for Biosocial Research* 2 (1981): 25–27. As quoted in James E. Gilliam and David

Unruh, "The Effects of Baker-Miller Pink on Biological, Physical and Cognitive Behaviour," *Journal of Orthomolecular Medicine* 3. no. 4 (1988): 202–206.

7.   A. G. Schauss, "Tranquilizing Effect of Color Reduces Aggressive Behavior and Potential Violence," *Journal of Orthomolecular Psychiatry* 8 (1979), 218–220; W. D. Wilson, *The Pink Relaxation Center/Study Carrel* (Gig Harbor, WA: Human Edge Systems, 1985). As quoted in Gilliam and Unruh, "The Effects of Baker-Miller Pink."

ACKNOWLEDGMENTS

❖

There are so many people to thank for their effort, guidance, and support of this book.

Thank you, Colette Baron-Reid, for your constant encouragement and the introduction to the Hay House family.

To everyone at Hay House, thank you for your dedication and the important role you play in bringing books to life. I'd specifically like to thank Patty Gift, Diane Ray, and Perry Crowe. The entire Hay House family has offered such a warm welcome, and I am honored to be part of this community.

To my editor, Lisa Cheng, your skillful guidance has been such a tremendous learning experience for me. I have so much gratitude for all of your support and hard work.

Lastly, there are several friends and colleagues who played a huge role in the early-stage development of this book. These are the people who were kind enough to read, edit, and offer guidance on the proposal and conception of *Your Life in Color*. In no particular order, thank you to Marilyn Kentz, Mariska Van Aalst, Ramey Warren, Alan Cohen, Danielle MacKinnon, James Van Praagh, Licia Morelli, and John Holland.

ABOUT THE AUTHOR

Photo of Dougall Fraser: © Kristin Klier

Dougall Fraser is an internationally recognized psychic, author, and cosmic coach. He utilizes color therapy, clairvoyance, intuition, empathy, interior design, and practical advice to help people assess and attain their goals and dreams. He was an invited speaker at OWN U, a live event series hosted by OWN, and has been featured on such shows as *Dr. Phil, The Real Housewives of O.C., Dancing with the Stars*, and *Good Day L.A.* He is a regular featured blogger for the *Huffington Post*, is the author of *But You Knew That Already*, and was the co-host of the late-night talk show *That Sex Show* for the LOGO network. He lives in Los Angeles with his husband, and you can visit him online at dougallfraser. com.

HAY HOUSE TITLES OF RELATED INTEREST

YOU CAN HEAL YOUR LIFE, the movie, starring Louise Hay & Friends
(available as a 1-DVD program and an expanded 2-DVD set)
Watch the trailer at: www.LouiseHayMovie.com

THE SHIFT, the movie,
starring Dr. Wayne W. Dyer
(available as a 1-DVD program and an expanded 2-DVD set)
Watch the trailer at: www.DyerMovie.com

❖   ❖   ❖

All of the above are available at your local bookstore,
or may be ordered by contacting Hay House.

❖   ❖   ❖

We hope you enjoyed this Hay House book. If you'd like to receive our online catalog featuring additional information on Hay House books and products, or if you'd like to find out more about the Hay Foundation, please contact:

Hay House, Inc., P.O. Box 5100, Carlsbad, CA 92018-5100
(760) 431-7695 or (800) 654-5126
(760) 431 6948 (fax) or (800) 650-5115 (fax)
www.hayhouse.com® • www.hayfoundation.org

❖ ❖ ❖

Published and distributed in Australia by: Hay House Australia Pty. Ltd., 18/36 Ralph St., Alexandria NSW 2015 • *Phone:* 612-9669-4299
Fax: 612-9669-4144 • www.hayhouse.com.au

Published and distributed in the United Kingdom by: Hay House UK, Ltd., Astley House, 33 Notting Hill Gate, London W11 3JQ • *Phone:* 44-20-3675-2450 • *Fax:* 44-20-3675-2451 • www.hayhouse.co.uk

Published and distributed in the Republic of South Africa by: Hay House SA (Pty), Ltd., P.O. Box 990, Witkoppen 2068 • info@hayhouse.co.za
www.hayhouse.co.za

Published in India by: Hay House Publishers India, Muskaan Complex, Plot No. 3, B-2, Vasant Kunj, New Delhi 110 070 • *Phone:* 91-11-4176-1620 • *Fax:* 91-11-4176-1630 • www.hayhouse.co.in

Distributed in Canada by: Raincoast Books, 2440 Viking Way, Richmond, B.C. V6V 1N2 • *Phone:* 1-800-663-5714 • *Fax:* 1-800-565-3770
www.raincoast.com

❖ ❖ ❖

Take Your Soul on a Vacation

Visit www.HealYourLife.com® to regroup, recharge,
and reconnect with your own magnificence.
Featuring blogs, mind-body-spirit news,
and life-changing wisdom from Louise Hay and friends.

Visit www.HealYourLife.com today!